DEDICATION

To my husband and my two sons ~ thank you for allowing me the time and space to heal and to fulfill my purpose in writing this book. I love you!

To my mother, who has always loved, encouraged and supported me; I love you more than words can express.

Thank you to each person who has impacted my life whether it was a good or a bad impact, it has made me into the person that I am today. Thank you for the deposits that you have made. I wouldn't change anything about my story.

Thank you Father God, for teaching me, loving me, healing and purposing me for your glory. You will always get the glory from my life!

Love, your beloved daughter!

TABLE OF CONTENTS

INTRODUCTION

Are you feeling stuck? Are you just going through the motions of life without enjoying it? Have you lost your joy and peace? Are you tired of wearing a mask, pretending like everything is ok? Are you tired and running out of ways to stay positive, knowing that deep down on the inside something is not right; something is missing?

Listen, "It's okay not to be okay."

If we were completely honest with ourselves, we all have felt this way at some point. What's not okay, is to keep going through life with a void; being broken, fearful, angry and wounded. At some point in life, we all will ask ourselves, "Is there more to this life than this?"

The trials of life can include a job loss, troubled relationships, broken homes, failed marriages; a wayward or sick child . These things can result in depression; hurt, pain and rejection. It can leave you feeling unworthy, undervalued; used, misused, mistreated and cheated. All of these and so much more cause deep wounds on our souls.

David said, "For my soul is full of troubles, and my life draws near to the grave. I am counted with those who go down to the pit; I am like a man who has no strength." Psalms 88:3-4 (NKJV)

We, too, face the trauma of our souls and sometimes we want to give up, but God who is the lover of our souls, wants to restore us. God does not see our condition as a failure like we do, but He sees it as an opportunity.

Being a broken vessel puts us in the perfect position to be emptied of ourselves and filled by God, for His purposes. A broken vessel does not equal an unusable vessel, it just means that vessel needs some tender loving care. God wants us to bring the shattered pieces of our soul to Him so that He can heal us, He is our Great Physician.

It's time to heal. There are wounds that you will never be able to see with your naked eye. They run deep and are bleeding all over every aspect of your life. Now is the time to allow yourself to be healed, be free, and enjoy life.

I have been in that position and it's hard to keep up the façade, pretending, like all is well. I suppressed my past hurts, fears, anxiety and rejections, avoiding the secrets of my past, which left me incapable of facing my present hurts. I had to stop to uncover my secret wounds. I needed to face my inner turmoil and my broken heart. Just as I had to stop to tend to my wounds, so do you.

Uncovering our secret wounds helps us to start the healing journey, by facing the things that we can't talk about and the things that we have ignored. When we hide our secret wounds, we place ourselves in a self-imposed prison, never free to thrive and live the abundant life that Jesus sacrificed for us to live.

Time does not heal wounds. Healing is a journey that does not happen overnight, but over time. It's an intentional process that takes a lot of commitment and effort. This journey is not for everyone, but for those who have a hunger in their soul for more of God. These people are not comfortable with living the status quo or a mediocre life. This journey is for those people who desire to be made whole and to live in peace with God and with themselves.

Our soul, our time, our peace and our joy are the most valuable and priceless items that we have in our possession.

Because you are reading this, you are ready to truly heal from your past and present soul wounds. The result will allow you to live a life full of abundance, love, peace, joy; walking in freedom, healed and delivered and thriving in your purpose.

In this book, I share my story and expose my wounds. I firmly believe that we do overcome by the blood of the Lamb and the words of our testimony. Our testimonies are meant to encourage other people through their trials. We may not have the same testimony, but we can learn from and be inspired by each other's stories.

God placed this book in my heart a long time ago. I'm so glad that it is now coming into fruition in this season. Writing this book, took me on a journey of healing, which allowed me to write from a place of love and not offense. I write this book out of the sincerity of my heart for people to feel the freedom and love of God that I have experienced. My desire is to see people healed, delivered, free and knowing who they are in Christ.

This book is filled with biblical principles, mixed with personal experiences that will help you identify the wounds in your soul. It will help you gain an understanding of why it's important to heal.

It's so important to heal well. In this book, you will find steps on how to heal and how to maintain your healing, so that you can find purpose for your pain and freedom to thrive in it.

This book is meant to help you start the journey to healing your soul wounds. There is a greater work that must be done in you and by you; your healing is totally dependent on your willingness to do the work. Don't be afraid to dig deeper. Healing is a life long journey, meaning we will always have levels and degrees of healing that we will always be going through, if we are intentional. Whatever your degree or level is, stay focused on your process and keep allowing God to do His work in you and through you.

Be confident in this very thing, that He who began a good work in you will carry it on to completion until the day of Christ Jesus. Philippians 1:6 (NKJV)

CHAPTER 1

SECRETS KILL

Keeping secrets is a normal part of our human nature; we are naturally wired to withhold certain things from others. Our parents have taught us from a very young age not to divulge our private information to other people. Our relationships are built on trust and our ability to keep what the people close to us deem as confidential information private. In relationships, the people who are close to us are privy to some of the most intimate details of our lives. Revealing guarded details about our past helps us to cultivate trust which connects us in a deeper, more intimate way.

So, are secrets good or bad? I don't think that there is one right answer to this question. However, I do believe determining whether a secret is good or bad has to be based on how you feel about that secret.

There are innocent things that we keep to ourselves which are very harmless. We generally deem those things as just private information. These innocent things don't make us feel anything and we give no second thought about them.

If the secret makes us feel good, joyful or excited, then these would be "good secrets". On the other hand, if the secret makes you feel shameful, anxious, stagnant or scared to tell then these would be negative secrets. While we all have secrets, if the secret is preventing you from living an abundant life that is free and peaceful than you are keeping a negative secret.

For nothing is hidden, except to be revealed; nor has anything been secret, but that it would come to light. Mark 4:22 (KJV)

Negative secrets are

- Hidden from everyone (done in the dark) - They affect you in an adverse way.
- They cause you to be silenced (muzzles your mouth)
- They fester (infecting you physically, mentally and emotionally).

- They torment you by replaying events, moments or thoughts over and over in your head.
- They cause self-hate, self-doubt, self-sabotage and confusion.
- Keeping unhealthy secrets can bring about sickness and disease.

Negative secrets are emotionally draining and can be devastating to a family. When you intentionally withhold information that can have a harmful effect on a person or group of people, it is unhealthy. When deciding whether to keep a secret we must ask ourselves, "Will this secret protect or hurt me or other individuals?"

There are several definitions for the word secret. I'll use the one from the Merriam Webster's dictionary because it coincides with the direction of this book. A secret is designed to elude observation or detection. It's meant to remain hidden; and to close mouths.

The devil uses negative secrets to torment us and to keep people from the truth. A negative secret cannot be properly dealt with until someone comes out and shines a light on the secret.

Secrets are festering places that the devil uses to torment us. He replays these negative thoughts and events to us over and over in our minds so that he can make accusations to and about us. The devil is the accuser of the brethren; he uses negative secrets to shame us and to make us feel guilty.

Negative secrets divide families, destroys trust and causes resentment. A negative secret can cause deep emotional scars, pain and even sickness. These secrets can cause life-altering problems to the person carrying around the secret.

Negative secrets are not of God. In John 8 verse 12, it tells us that Jesus is the light of the world, whoever follows him will never walk in darkness, but will have the light of life. Negative secrets are usually kept hidden and will cause negative consequences to our spiritual, physical, emotional health; and in our relationships.

Real intimacy in relationships requires us to be open, honest and transparent; when we carry a negative secret it does not allow us to do this. Instead, we will live a life that is guarded, never allowing people to get close to us. Negative secrets hinder spiritual freedom and prevent us from living an abundant life filled with peace and joy.

Keeping a negative secret can be stressful, some things aren't easy to keep to yourself. Lying to your family and friends can be a major source of anxiety.

Effects of keeping a negative secret can cause:

- Stress, depression and anxiety
- Shame, guilt and mistrust
- Addictions
- Isolation
- Self-sabotage
- Self-hate
- Self-protection
- Dysfunctional relationships (broken homes and generational curses)
- Unfulfilled purpose and aborted dreams
- Sickness and disease
- Mental illness
- Suicide

Studies have shown that it's not the stress of hiding the secret from people, but it is the stress of thinking about the secret all the time, that is burdensome. We are not supposed to carry heavy burdens (things that are oppressive and worrisome), instead we are to release our burdens to find rest and peace. If this secret does not give you peace, then it's a burden.

Come unto me, all who are weary and carry heavy burdens, and I will give your rest. Matthew 11:28 (NLT)

The average person is keeping an average of 13 secrets right now; five of them are secrets they've never told anyone. Some of the most common types of secrets being kept are about:

- Finances (bankruptcy; job loss or lying about income to keep up with the Joneses)
- Hidden relationship (adultery or cheating)
- Addictions (illegal or prescription drug abuse; sexual addictions)
- Alternative lifestyles
- Abortion
- Trauma
- Family secrets

The list could go on and on and can range from not being honest about your real feelings with a significant other, to hiding criminal activities and/or harming someone.

So, how do you decide if a secret is worth telling?

It doesn't matter if the secret is big or small; it's more important to assess how the secret makes you feel. We must ask the hard questions, especially those concerning our childhood. In the case of childhood trauma, you must ponder these questions, "Is this trauma dominating my thoughts and hindering my ability to open up and be intimate in relationships? Am I making bad decisions as a result of the trauma that I faced as a child? Will keeping this secret cause me to harm myself or someone else? Do I find myself wanting be open and honest about this secret at times but it's too difficult? If your answer is yes, it is worth talking to a counselor, religious advisor, mentor or a trustworthy friend.

Some people will find it difficult to verbalize their secret and may find it easier to write it down in a journal, then allow someone who is trustworthy to read it. The point is just to get it out.

Telling someone for the first time can be very scary, difficult and emotional; but it is also very freeing. Releasing your secret will start the healing process and shut the mouth of the accuser. Remember a part of the definition for secrets is to "close one's mouth," to make you silent or to prevent you from speaking your truth. When we tell our truth, it disarms the enemy and strips him of the power that he had over us.

You have power on the inside of you, and you activate that power when you speak. Be bold, be courageous and speak your truth; remove the muzzle from your mouth and be free.

How do we combat negative secrets? We open our mouths and we speak our truth to expose the secret.

Ephesians 5:11 (NKJV) gives us some reassurance, it says, "Have nothing to do with fruitless deeds of darkness but rather expose them." Ephesian 5:12 from the Message Bible says, "It's a scandal when people waste their lives on things they must do in the darkness where no one will see. Rip the covers off those fraudulent things and see how attractive they look in the light of Christ."

It is for our benefit that hidden secrets be exposed, so that the light of truth can shine on us to help us heal.

Why do we keep negative secrets?

As stated previously, not all secrets are bad or negative, only the ones that affect us in an unhealthy way or cause us to be silenced, afraid to speak the truth.

Sometimes, we keep negative secrets to keep the peace in relationships, because we don't want to hurt other people's feelings. We want to protect ourselves from other people's perceptions of us. No one likes to feel judged or humiliated. We think because judgment, shame and guilt from others is just too hard to bear. Unfortunately, we are harder on ourselves then other people are. We judge ourselves pretty severely and belittle our worth for every little mistake, even things we had no control over.

Most of us keep negative secrets because we are afraid that if we tell the truth, it would prove that we are unworthy, unlovable or dirty. In our minds, we think that telling our negative secret somehow tells the world that we are broken, damaged, and unfixable; and that we are bad people. But the truth is, we are all wounded and broken in some capacity. We are not alone; and in reality, there is someone out there who has been through what we are going through.

The devil uses this lie and others to shame us and to keep us from speaking our truth. This is why all negative secrets ***must*** be uncovered.

Depression, the secret killer

Depression is the loss of feeling of pleasure (joy or happiness); hopelessness; extreme sadness; loss of appetite and feelings of guilt and shame. Looking at this definition, we all have experienced a form of depression at least once in our lives. So why is it hard for us to have a discussion about depression? Society has made having depression and any mental illnesses, a stigma. We can feel like something is wrong with us or that we are broken. As a result, we hide our pain due to our inability to process it and we secretly use medication, illegal drugs, sex and/ or food (overeating) to numb the pain that we are feeling.

Depression has become an epidemic in America, 1 out of 9 Americans are on medication for depression; 1 out of 5 have been on medication for depression in the past. Every other commercial on television is talking about how you can be prescribed medication to manage depression. This is a serious issue that needs to be addressed, but most people can't and will not speak about depression because of the reactions of other people.

Most people who are secretly depressed, suffer in silence. This is a tool of the enemy to pull you deeper into darkness and more and more into isolation. He uses isolation to pull you away from family and friends, so that he can torment you with accusations. In isolation, feelings of depression and, hopelessness creep in. The enemy can make you think that suicide is the best solution.

A secret held for too long becomes a self - imposed prison. This is why, we must release these things that are or have been harmful to us. Expressing your feelings, by talking is the best therapy that humans have; getting a different perspective on the matter can be especially beneficial.

Suicide is making a permanent decision from a temporary situation. We all have emotions and sometimes those emotions overwhelm us. Know that suicide is **never** the answer. The enemy loves to remind us of our past and torment us with our present state; but he has no knowledge of our future. So don't give into the lies he tries to whisper to you. When we expose our own secrets, we take away his ammunition, so that he has no bullets to fire at us.

Even the great Apostle Paul and so many others in the Bible have suffered with this. The early Christians were being persecuted and even martyred for their beliefs. Paul expresses his frustrations in 2 Corinthians 1:8 (NASB) by saying, "We were burdened excessively, beyond our strength, so that we despaired even life," He felt hopeless about life.

The burdens of life can weigh us down; the dissatisfactions with work and marriage; the loss of a loved one; traumas and injustices, added with trying to make ends meet, can be all too much, at times. Jesus tells us to come to Him, all who are weary and heavy laden, He says, "I will give you rest, learn from me, for I am gentle and humble in heart and you will find rest for your souls, for my burden is light." (Matthew 11:28 NASB)

We can lay our burdens at the feet of Jesus, because they are too heavy for us to bear. We should cast all our anxiety on Him, because He cares for us; when we do, He helps and sustains us.

If you are having thoughts of suicide, please do not think that you have to handle this alone, seek help. The devil's job is to steal, kill and destroy. He wants to exterminate you; but if he can get you to do it, that's even better. Please don't give in to the lies he is using to make you feel like things will never get better. There is always hope in tomorrow. Hope is a joyful expectation of the future.

Tomorrow is a new day. It's another chance to start over again. It's filled with new mercy and grace to carry you through any and everything you will encounter. You are important and necessary in this life; don't give up and don't give in. Hang in there. It gets better.

National Suicide Prevention Lifeline @1-800-273-8255

When we uncover our secrets, it frees us from our self-imposed prisons and opens the door to healing and being authentic to ourselves and the people that we love.

Uncovering our secrets can make us feel naked and vulnerable; it takes a lot of courage to speak our truth, but the reward of freedom is so worth it. Accepting yourself with all your flaws is an act of freedom and self-love. You can't heal what you aren't willing to confront. Uncover your secret wounds, so that you can heal.

CHAPTER 2

MY SECRET WOUNDS

As a little girl, I was taught to respect my elders, be obedient to adults and to go to an adult if something bad happened. Adults are supposed to protect children, provide for them, teach them and provide a nurturing and safe environment. What happens when an adult is the one who is doing harm to a child? What do you do when it's someone you trust?

I was nine when my mother's boyfriend began molesting me. I can't remember all of the details about what happened during that time; and the things I do remember are a little scattered. I believe my mind went into a self-protection mode so that I could move forward with my life. Parts of my memory have come back to me, little by little, and the more I think on that time in my life the more the memories come flooding back.

My mother and father were never married, and my father took no active involvement in raising us, other than paying child support. He never took us around his family; and early on he denied that we were his children. So, I had no idea how a father-daughter relationship was supposed to be.

I can remember wanting a "daddy," so when this man came around, I trusted him. I was a very obedient child, so when any adult told me to do something, I did it. He treated me special and he told me to keep our "secret."

A little while after meeting him, my mother moved with him to Minnesota. I can remember it was very cold there and there was a lot of snow in the winter. I can remember standing outside waiting on the school bus in mounds of snow. Minnesota's winters were bone chillingly cold. The air had a distinctive smell that I can still smell whenever I go back, till this day.

Shortly after we moved, my mother had to go take care of business, so she left us with the boyfriend. I remember we were sitting on the floor in the living room, watching TV. He called me to come into the bathroom with him. I remember him picking me up and sitting me on the sink as he was talking to me. I didn't feel scared. I must have felt comfortable enough to go into the bathroom with him. I can remember him talking to me at first and then he exposed his penis to me. Then he touched me, and he had me touch him. After that, I do not remember what happened or how I felt.

I realize now, that I blacked out to withdraw physically and emotionally from what was happening to my body. Dissociation is a normal defense mechanism that happens during a traumatic experience to numb us and to avoid the memories of events.

There were 5 of us, four boys and I'm the only girl. The apartment that we moved into only had two bedrooms; so there weren't enough rooms. The boys got one room and my mother got the other. We had a long storage closet that became my room; I had a bed and I think I had a dresser; so it worked, and it was mine. I was happy.

By this time, the molestation had escalated to penetration. No one knew what was happening, because he would come in the middle of the night when everyone was asleep. One night, I decided toroll myself into my sheets to protect myself (I thought this would stop him); but it didn't work, he just picked me up, carried me to the living room floor behind the couch in the dark. I remember him putting his hand over my mouth, as he had his way. I will not go into grave details about what happened but I do remember snippets of what he did on the floor in the dark, behind the couch.

I didn't know how to verbalize what was happening. This was back in the eighties, when there was no internet and kids were innocent about sex. All we knew was that we couldn't watch the rated R movies. If we happened to be watching a movie with our parents that showed any nudity, we were trained to cover our eyes and if it was too much, we couldn't watch it at all.

I guess I was scared to tell because I thought that in some way, I caused this to happen and that my mom wouldn't believe me. He said, "no one would believe me." He also made promises and bribes; he brought me the Cabbage Patch doll I wanted. She was a white Cabbage Patch kid with light brown yarn hair and I named her "Melissa."

I don't believe that my childhood was bad. In elementary school, I had friends and a boy that liked me. I think I liked him as well. I was in the third or fourth grade, it was nothing serious. I was a part of the videography program there at the school, which I enjoyed. I can still remember this one Christmas, it was crazy.

We had toys everywhere. I remember each one of us had a pile of toys. We didn't always have everything, but my mother made sure we always had something. She still does that till this day, it's funny. As a single mother of five kids, it was hard for her to make ends meet and still get us what we wanted. At that time I'm sure the boyfriend was helping my mother take care of us, as well.

I can remember having good times at home. My mother and her boyfriend would make homemade cookies and pizza for us. I even remember when the boyfriend let us taste beer for the first time. It looked like pee and it was disgusting. Because of that exposure, I have never liked beer or the taste of alcohol. When I did have something to drink, it was in very small moderation; but I never got drunk.

How did I tell?

As I look back over my life, I can now see the hand of God giving me instructions even in this situation.

I finally realized that my mother's boyfriend's behavior was wrong, and I had to tell. I also now realize that I had help telling my mother, by the Holy Spirit. I can remember wanting to tell her, but I was afraid. I didn't think that I was brave enough to say it. So the Holy Spirit set everything up and all I had to do was speak up.

My mother and I were sitting on the couch in the living room, watching TV and "ironically," we were watching a lifetime movie about a little girl being molested. When the scene came, in which the little girl was telling her mother what happened to her, I felt embolden and before I knew it, the words came out of my mouth. I can't even remember the words that I said to my mother, but I do remember her reaction and response, she believed me right away. A heavy weight had been lifted off of my chest and I was finally free!

The little girl on TV showed me how to tell and she gave me the words to speak; she was bold enough to tell her story. She gave me the strength and courage to tell my mother everything. For many years, I held on to the fact that my mother believed me; it meant the world to me.

My story isn't special and there are many people who have a similar or worst stories to tell. I just decided not to be a victim any longer and to never be silenced again.

The devil manipulated me; he stole my innocence and he tried to destroy my future. So I have made it my purpose in life to destroy the works of the enemy by exposing the schemes and tactics he uses to destroy lives.

When I told my mother, I uncovered what was hidden in the dark to expose it in the light. Speaking up stopped the sexual abuse and it freed me from not being able to sleep safely in my bed, at night. I now realize that even back then I had power in my mouth to speak the truth. When I opened my mouth, I destroyed the works of the enemy; the Bible says, "We overcome by the blood of the Lamb and the words of our testimony." When I decided not to be afraid or silenced by the secret I was keeping, I took my power back from the enemy. I took away his permission to torment me about something that I had no control over.

Keeping my secret was keeping me bound to a sin that was committed against me. This was not my sin, nor my shame, but the devil tried to use it against me by making me feel it was.

Guilt and shame feed secrets and secrets feed guilt and shame. The devil has been using these tactics since the beginning of time. In John 4, the people in the town of Samaria shamed the woman at the well. We see isolation and shame used with the woman with the issue of blood in Luke 8:43. And we see guilt and shame with King David when he took another man's wife, impregnated her and then he had her husband killed in battle to cover up his sin, in 2 Samuel 12. As you can see, guilt and shame will creep in whether you did something wrong or if you are a victim of circumstances. The devil will use anything that he can to twist the truth and present us with a lie; he is the father of lies and the truth is not in him.

Guilt will make you feel bad about your behavior. Shame makes you feel bad about yourself. I went through a process of feeling like being molested was my fault (guilt); I felt dirty and I felt like everyone could see "my secret" (shame). This was a lie. I now know and understand that being sexually abused was not my fault; and I also know that no-one could see that I was being sexually abused. This is was a trick of the devil used to twist what I thought about myself and how I thought other's perceived me.

Sexual abuse devastated me. It defiled me and stole my innocence. I used to think to myself, "Am I a virgin?" I really didn't know. It made me feel ashamed, numb and dead on the inside. It stole my joy and as a result, I became angry and bitter.

After I told my mother about the abuse, we moved back home. There was no counseling and no talking about what happened. I was just left to deal with all my feelings; and yet again, I had to keep another secret. This left me feeling alone and isolated because I still wasn't free to talk about what happened. It wasn't that I really wanted to talk about it, but I think it would have really helped. I had no way to express all the feelings that were bottled up on the inside of me; I still wasn't free.

As I mentioned before, secrets are festering places that the devil uses to torment us. Fester means to become infected; rot and get worse and more intense, over a long period of time. When we allow secrets to fester, they infect every part of our lives mentally, physically, spiritually and emotionally.

Physically, I didn't like myself. I thought I was too skinny and too dark. I didn't like to look at myself in the mirror and I definitely didn't like other people, especially men looking at me. I was hiding myself under baggy clothes, so that I wouldn't draw attention to myself. I was very self-conscious; I didn't even like showing my legs.

One day, my mother wanted me to wear a skirt to school and I just felt so uncomfortable; so I decided to wear a pair of leggings underneath my skirt. I had the leggings rolled under my skirt until I left the house. As I started on my way to school, I started pulling the leggings down. What I didn't realize was that she was watching me in the door. She called me back to the house to take them off.

I was ashamed of my body, I didn't like being the center of attention. I suffered with self-hate, fear and anxiety which made it hard to make friends and maintain healthy relationships. I was quiet, shy and very stubborn. I was very aware of my surroundings and very suspicious of everyone, especially men.

As I grew older, my mother started sending us to church; I finally had a safe place. I latched on to the word of God. I do not remember where I got my first Bible, but it was this little orange New Testament Bible. The wording in it was really small, but I would sit in my room, reading it. I loved reading. Reading gave me the ability to escape my own thoughts and enter into another reality. I loved reading so much that I would read the backs of lotions bottles, air freshener and cleaning products. I read whatever I could get my hands on. My favorite place to read was in the bathroom because it was quiet and warm.

I was about thirteen or fourteen when I told my story again, it was to the Pastor's wife. She had a similar story, so I felt safe because she was open and honest about her past. My aunt also told me her story. These women took time out to listen to my story, they validated my feelings and they told me, "It was not your fault! You were an innocent child." We bonded, especially my aunt and

I. I finally had someone who I could be totally honest with; my healing began.

My counseling wasn't the usual professional type of counseling, but more of spiritual healing activated by God's love. I remember the Pastor's wife would sing this song about King David called Shepherd Boy by Ray Boltz, I could identify with David; he was the underdog; isolated in the field with the sheep, he was overlooked, underestimated and rejected; he was not expected to be chosen to be king, it sounded familiar to me.

The words of the song were powerful and when she would sing it, it was like she was singing to me.

Shepherd Boy

Words and Music by Ray Boltz and Steve Millikan:

"When others see a shepherd boy, God may see a king even though your life seems filled with ordinary things. In just a moment he can touch you and everything will change, when others see a shepherd boy God may see a king." The words of this song changed my life. I felt like, Wow! He sees me and He can change my life with just one touch. I wanted that. I felt the love of Father God for the first time and I feel in love with Him and his word.

You see God doesn't look at the outward appearance, He looks at the heart. The Lord began to tell me how much he loved me. He told me that I was fearfully and wonderfully made and that I had a purpose in this world. He became my refuge and I soaked up everything He taught me.

When other kids were outside playing, I was spending time with God (as I write this I can see where our relationship started). No one understood this, especially not my mother. She would kick me out of the house and call me a "hermit." She wanted me to go make friends and be a "regular kid;" but I wasn't regular. I enjoyed going outside to a certain extent and I had friends, but it wasn't like being with God. You see, God didn't judge me. I didn't have to try to fit in or prove I was worthy of friendship; I could be me.

I struggled with fitting in and trying to get acceptance from people. How could I expect others to accept me when I didn't accept myself? As I grew up, I still had to deal with the wounds from being sexually abused, but I had God and I was trying to walk the straight and narrow. I got involved in church and things were going well. I had finally gotten to a point where I didn't think about the abuse anymore.

As a child of sexual abuse, I was thirty-five percent more likely to be sexually abused again. There were several attempts, but nothing on the scale of the molestation at age nine. I had an older female cousin who tried to make me perform a sexual act on her (this may have been before the molestation).

Then, I had an uncle who came into the room with alcohol on his breath, he grabbed my breast and squeezed them, saying, "Give me some milk." I never told because I thought I was dreaming until another child came forward saying that he did something to her. Then I knew it was real.

By the time I was in the seventh or eighth grade, my mother and father rekindled their relationship, which took my mother away from our home. He wouldn't even come in to see us, most of the time. He would blow his horn and she would go. My older brother and I became more responsible for our younger siblings, cooking, homework and getting them ready for school.

One day, I had to go pick up my younger brother from elementary school, my younger brother under me walked with me. As we were leaving the school, I saw an older boy that went to my school. But I didn't know him personally. He came up to me, grabbing me wanting me to kiss him, I refused and pushed him off of me. He started beating me up. He hit me in my face and as I fell to the ground, then he started hitting me on top of my head. Luckily, a woman who was driving by in her car stopped him and gave us a ride home. My mother and I went to principal's office, the next morning. I believe he was suspended from school, but I never saw him again.

I was tired, and I grew more and more angry. I told myself that I had to toughen up; so I began to fight. I had several fights in school. I was tired of people abusing me. I was mad. I would say harsh things to people. I purposely had a mean look on my face to keep people from getting to close. I didn't care about anybody's feelings because no-one cared about mine. I did not like people. I began to avoid people. I felt no one could be trusted.

Rejected, Accepted, Rejected!

I think that every human being longs to belong to something or someone. It's just the way that God created us; this is why he created family. My relationship with my father was non-existent, in the beginning. We were acquainted with each other and he had finally accepted us as his children, but our relationship never grew into an intimate relationship. It was not from a lack of effort; time just wasn't on our side.

When I was a little girl, he visited us, but it wasn't on a regular basis. He called us his "little people," but I had the name "princess." My father was a big guy; a handsome marine. My brothers and I would wrestle with him. He would make a muscle and we would try to wrestle him down to try to deflate his muscle.

I believe that my father and mother did the best that they could considering the circumstances, after all we were his "outside kids." When we met our older brother for the first time, he had on his army uniform. He was on active duty in the Gulf War; it was cool having an older brother. He accepted us. My older brother always tried to include us. Where my father failed, he stepped in to try to bridge the gap; but my father's side of the family never accepted us, especially my half-sister.

I longed for a big sister, then I found out I had a big sister; I was excited only to realize that she would never accept me/us. As a little girl, I remember being at my aunt's house and hearing the doorbell ring; and it was her, my sister. I knew she was my sister, but she never acknowledged or spoke a word to me and that has not changed since then. Weird, right?

Anyway, before my father had his stroke, we were working on our relationship. I remember going out to dinner for my birthday with him for the first time. There were times when he would give me a ride to work and from work. When I had my sons, I would take them over to his house to visit and he was very helpful in picking up my oldest son from school.

One day, he was found unconscious in his house, he had a brain hemorrhage/a stroke. They had to do surgery to relieve the pressure off of his brain, it was touch and go, but he pulled through. He was paralyzed on one side. After his first stroke, I went to see my father occasionally. I didn't want to intrude in my sister's space and honestly I didn't think he remembered me, anyway.

A few years later, I remember getting a call at work from my older brother saying that my father was being taken to the hospital, again. I thought it was his blood pressure because he wasn't taking his pill like he was supposed to. My brother sounded calm on the phone, so I didn't think anything of it. I told him to let me know what's going on. I received another call from my brother, saying that they were moving my father to another hospital and that he had another stroke, but this time it wasn't looking good. My heart sank. I didn't know what to do. I told my co-worker. She asked me if I was going to go to the hospital and I was like I don't know, being that we weren't welcomed by his family. I just didn't know how to feel about all of that. So, I reached out to my two brothers (my mother and father had two son's and one daughter together), to see what they thought. As always, we decided to go as a united front. As we walked into the hospital, and past a waiting room, I heard, "They not gone even speak". I was with my younger brother at the time and neither one of us have a problem with saying what was on our minds. But I went into big sister mode, so that things didn't escalate. I went into the room spoke to everybody then continued down the hall, reminding my brother that we have one mission to complete and that was to pay respect to our father.

The day my father was taken off of life support was difficult and awkward, being in close proximity with people who we knew didn't accept us. By this point, our only goal was to honor the man, we called our father. My brother made a way for us to have some time alone with our father. There was so much anger. We had so many unanswered questions; we were left in this mess that my father created.

That night, my father was taken off of life support, I tried to comfort him as he gasped for air. It was too painful to watch. After about an hour or so, we decided to leave; but my older brother stayed. I asked him to call me when it was over. That night in the parking lot of the hospital, my brothers and I comforted each other and made an agreement that after all this was over, we would close the door to this chapter in our lives.

My father lasted until three a.m. He was such a fighter. The man that we knew as our "father," was no more. I wept then I called my mother to see how she was. After all, my mother and father were still together up until he got sick. Needless to say, she was devastated.

We were left out of all the funeral arrangements. My mother was left out in the cold and we were even left out of the obituary; rejected yet again. We were livid. My mother decided that she wasn't going to the funeral. My brothers were only going, if I was going. And oh, yes, I was going, so I thought. I wanted to go so that I could give each and every one of them a piece of my mind, but God.

God has always told me to protect my integrity, at all costs, I didn't know why, but it was very important to Him that I didn't smear my name. I went to view my father at the funeral home, but I did not attend my father's funeral. After that, I was done with my father's family.

Seeking Love in Men!

I was subconsciously looking for acceptance and love from other people; a love that I never received from my father. So the first man that came along showing interest in me, made me feel good. I felt like, okay, I am attractive to someone. I am loveable. I was so flattered that it didn't take long for me to fall into what I now know as lust.

I was a junior in high school, working in a restaurant in the evenings so that I could help my mother pay bills and get some of the things that I wanted. I was a good student in school. I stayed on the honor roll up until my junior year in high school. I always knew that I wanted to go into healthcare because I loved helping people.

I met my sons' father working at the restaurant. His mother was a co-worker. I guess he saw me, one night, that he came to pick her up. He told his mother he thought that I was cute and was interested in me. He asked his mother to ask me if we could meet. So, we did. He was cute, so we exchanged numbers and started talking.

I was responsible for finding my way back and forth to work because my mother never learned how to drive. I would catch the bus during the day and then I would have to find a ride home, at night. He offered to take me to work and pick me up whenever he could, which was a great relief.

I started skipping school to go see him. I was a novice who got caught the very first time that I skipped. We decided to go to the flea market and the person who was taking us was a family friend. He told my mother and of course she was upset, and told me not to do it again. I should have listened, but I was being rebellious and I thought I knew what was best for me.

He didn't live that far from us. He actually lived along the route that I walked to go to school, so I would just make a detour to his house. He was a couple years older than me, so I knew he was home. I felt wanted and accepted by him, so eventually we started having sex; it wasn't anything spectacular but once you open that door it becomes a natural part of the relationship.

Something didn't feel right, though. He had this female "friend," that would be over his house. She would pick up his mother from work at night and from time to time, she would also give me a ride home. I didn't think anything of it, at first. Eventually I found out that they were more than "friends" and that she was pregnant by him. I was devastated and felt betrayed, not only by my boyfriend, but by his mother. She knew about all the other females he was dealing with when she introduced us. So, I left him alone. I started dating another guy, but in the midst of all of this, I found out that I was pregnant. So I left the other guy alone and told my sons' father the news.

By this time, I was eighteen and just starting my senior year in high school. One day, I was cleaning my closet in my bedroom and my mother came in and she asked me if I was still skipping school? "Uh-oh", I thought. I knew I couldn't lie to her. I said, "Yes," I don't remember what was said after that, but she looked disappointed in me. I didn't understand because when I was trying to be a good girl, going to church, focused on God, it wasn't enough. I actually remember my mother telling me that she and my father thought that I was "gay," because I wasn't interested in boys at that time. So, I just felt like, there was no pleasing her. Now that I was being "normal," and it still was not enough.

Our relationship during my teenaged years was not good, because I didn't feel like I could talk to my mother about my feelings. Any way back to the point; I'm so glad that I told my mother the truth because a little while later, I had to break the news to her that I was pregnant. Her response was, "You better get rid of it. We don't need another mouth to feed in here," So, I started saving money to get an abortion. Then one day, she came into my room and asked me what my plan was. I said, "I'm saving money so that I can get an abortion," she said, "I really didn't mean that because I don't believe in abortions." I was shocked! She wanted me to keep the baby. She said we would work it out; so that's what we did. Side note: Although, I didn't get an abortion this time, that thought was planted and became my first response later in my life. The seed was planted.

Being pregnant in high school was so embarrassing and shameful, no-body expected to see me, 'the good girl', pregnant; but I was. I can still remember some of my teachers' faces to this day.

I was always determined to defy the odds. I told them that I'm going to finish high school and attend college so that I could take care of my son, their response was "Yeah, sure you are." I did everything that I signed up for my senior year, which included going to clinicals for my CNA certificate. I graduated from high school as a certified nursing assistant; and the following week I gave birth to my son.

After my son's birth, I got refocused. I worked and attended classes at the community college, but I struggled and eventually had to stop going. My son's father wasn't in his life and he has never helped with anything. My brothers and my mother were such a good support system for us with babysitting, helping to supply what he needed. We worked as a team.

By the time my son was four, I was lonely. I went out on a date with a co-worker's brother. He just wasn't my type. Now, I'm not saying he wasn't attractive because he was a nice looking man, but he just wasn't someone I would have "normally" been attracted to. He was very persuasive, relentless, charming and passionate. He was a few years older than me and had a job, so I just decided to go with the flow, just to see what happens. This was my first real grown-up relationship; and it started off amazing. Let's just say he taught me a lot.

Around that time, I decided that I wanted my own space. So I did find a place close to where he lived in lower income housing. I ended up pregnant at twenty-two. I was disappointed with the course that my life was on and also with myself. I felt like I was a failure, I had become a statistic. I was an unwed mother with one child and one on the way, no degree and living in the low - income housing. I was thoroughly disgusted and disappointed with in myself and in denial about being pregnant. I became depressed, angrier, unmotivated and trapped. By this time, my relationship with God was non-existent and I was nowhere near the vision that God had given me for my life; it was like I was on a vicious declining cycle that I couldn't get off of.

My second pregnancy had a lot of complications. I was sick all the time and I developed preeclampsia. I also dilated prematurely, so they had to put a pessary in place to prevent me from going into premature labor.

The relationship was okay, he was with me every step of the way. He made sure we had everything that we needed, but I just wasn't happy or satisfied. Something was missing. As I reflect, it wasn't necessarily him, it was me.

We had our son, he came at thirty-four weeks, he was so tiny, but healthy. My oldest son was in love with his little brother. I was done having kids at twenty-three, but my doctor refused to tie my tubes. Two kids was enough for me. I ended up pregnant again, but I had a miscarriage, I thought whew, I dodged a bullet. Then it happened again and we decided to get an abortion.

My life was out of order. My decision making was flawed, I went into a deeper depression, I was in a dark place. Nothing and no one could make me happy. I remember on my twenty-third birthday, I was at my mother's house and it should have been a happy day, but it wasn't. I was sitting on the couch in the living room crying and my oldest son asked me, "Mommy, why are you crying?" I didn't know why I was crying but I was just sad.

God had shown me a vision of my life as a child. In this vision, I was married; my husband and I were influential people in the community and we had two children. As a little girl, I wanted to be a pediatrician. So in my vision, I thought we were doctors. I always knew God had a plan for my life. I just didn't know exactly how it would come to fruition. As I sat there on my mother's couch crying, I felt like that vision was so far away, that it was unattainable. But God is faithful!

By this time, I was at least attending my old church. I knew where I could go to be filled up, but I wasn't faithful to God. I was sabotaging my relationship with my son's father because I remembered that vision God had shown me and this was not it. I had failed God. I was unworthy of his love and forgiveness. It's crazy because I wasn't a party girl so that never was my problem but I had fallen into a generational cycle of fornicating, having children outside of marriage, working, but needing public assistance, living in low income housing and at that time I had no interest in getting married.

Why would I get married? My mother never married. My aunt never married. So I didn't feel the need for marriage. Crazy, right?! My youngest son's father wanted to get married but I just wasn't interested in any of that. It was foolish thinking on my part. Our relationship was not going well. I found out that he was cheating on me and had a son with someone else. I forged a plan to move out of the relationship. I went down to the child support office so that I could petition for child support. I told him that my case worker was pushing me to seek child support.

On our court day, we rode together in my car, a united front, right? We got into the courtroom and the judge started asking questions. I didn't lie, I told the truth. I looked over at my son's father. He was crying because he had to pay child support. I guess he felt that he was doing his part and that he didn't need to be forced to do so. He was good about making sure our son had what he needed, but I didn't like the fact that I had to ask him for money. It was the right thing to do, besides I didn't want anyone controlling how I went about taking care of business. It was a part of my exit strategy.

I had been at the restaurant for almost 10 years and I was having a hard time finding work in the medical field. I tried working at a nursing home but that was not for me. That only lasted for 3 months and back to the restaurant, I went. My sister in-law got me an interview at a doctor's office and I got the job as a medical assistant without the certificate. That was God. I was finally able to leave the restaurant, move out of the low income housing, and broke up with my son's father. I just deserved better.

While all of this was going on, I was still a working mother who had to take care of her sons. My youngest was about three years old when I took him to the health department for vaccinations.

Later that day, I noticed that he wasn't feeling good and he had a fever of 104 degrees. For three days we took him back and forth to the ER. The fever would go down, but then it spiked again. They couldn't find anything wrong; it was the weirdest thing. Then finally the fever broke, but my son was never the same after that. Before the vaccination he was a busy body, always getting into things; he was talking as well as a three year old could. But after this set of vaccinations, he regressed. He wouldn't make eye contact. He liked playing by himself. He would rock and do repetitive behaviors. I asked his father if he noticed anything different about him, he said no; but something just wasn't right.

I enrolled him into preschool, I thought maybe he needs to be around other kids his age. One day, the preschool called me in and told me that I needed to take him to be tested. I did and I didn't think anything of it because I had my suspicions anyway. The diagnoses was Autism. I asked, "What is that and what do we need to do to get him healed from it?" They said, "It's not something that can be healed," I was devastated and lost. No parent wants to hear devastating news about their baby, especially things that will affect their entire life. I didn't know what to do, I began to cry out to God. "Lord, what do I do with this information? Lord, why my child? Lord, are you serious? I can't do this, Lord."

I would get calls from the school, they wanted to put him in special education classes. We had to have a meeting to set up his Individualized Education Program (IEP). When we get to the meeting, his regular teacher is there also. She makes the statement, "I don't believe he will ever be able to learn or be a functional person in this society." Oh, it was on, I could have reached across the table and snatched a hole in that teacher. I told her not mine. I made a declaration even though I didn't know it at the time, "He will be a functional adult. He will graduate high school, He will go to college and he will live an abundant life." I never saw that teacher ever again, but I do know that she wasn't teaching there anymore.

God sent a special education teacher who was awesome. Her son had severe Autism while mine had a mild case of autism called Pervasive Developmental Disorder (NOS). She taught me how to deal with his behaviors. He didn't like loud sounds. It was harder to potty train him, and he got into all kinds of things. He needed to be watched closely, he didn't learn like his brother, but he was extremely smart but stubborn. It was a very stressful and trying season as a single mother.

I was working in the doctor's office, thank God, they were very flexible. They would allow me time to go pick up my son from school to take him to my mother's. Sometimes I had to miss work because of his behavior; I needed a break.

I started missing my relationship with my son's father and having someone around. We had sex occasionally but he didn't want to get back together, which left me in despair, broken, alone, depressed and frustrated. I remember thinking what is wrong with you? Why would you want someone who you didn't want a future with you and who cheated on you? As much as I should have stopped to answer these questions, I didn't. I just kept moving, right into the next relationship without skipping a beat.

One day, I was bringing groceries into the house and here comes this big white dog came running across the street and before I knew it my youngest son took off running up the stairs and the dog chased him into the house; I screamed at the man, "You better get your dog, before I do." He thought it was funny, but it wasn't. My outlet came in the form of a tall, handsome man and to top it off my brother moved in with me. It was perfect, now I had a live-in babysitter. I thought, "Lord, you are so faithful." Twisted thinking, right?!

I started seeing this man, he was very helpful and attentive to my needs. We would go out on dates or just hang out. It was nice to have someone who was interested in me for a change.

I rented the house for just one year. The landlord was crazy. It was weird, she was always somewhere around trying to gain access to the house, besides that I just couldn't afford to pay rent and utilities. I also wanted my sons to go to a better school district. So, we moved into a two-bedroom apartment with a lake view. Things were good; the boys transitioned pretty well. My oldest son got into a little trouble here and there, because of his smart mouth; but the youngest quickly adjusted. I was attending church on a regular basis, but I felt like it was time to move on from my childhood church. I decided to visit this church that had a reputation. I would not have considered it, but I kept running into some of the members of this church and they were so sweet, faith-filled and proud of their church. The first couple of visits were amazing, so I said to my sons, "If we go this third time and we like it, we are going to join" And of course, it was amazing. We joined and I rededicated my life to Christ. I had never heard this kind of teaching but it was just what I needed at the time. They offered classes on understanding your Bible, marriage; Christian finance, the end times and so many other options. I was at home because I loved to learn about God and I wanted that foundation for my sons.

Relationship wise, something wasn't right; he would disappear for days without communication and then he would pop-up like everything was okay. I understood that he had a job that required him to travel but something was amiss. I was in limbo, waiting and hoping that this would be the man that I would spend the rest of my life with, yes marriage. While attending this church, I learned about the covenant of marriage. I wanted to get married and I expressed this to my man. He was shocked and maybe disappointed because he was comfortable with me not wanting to get married. I was understanding with him since he had already been married twice before. So, I guess I wouldn't want to get married again either, so I didn't force the issue. We moved forward and then (uh-oh), I started feeling nauseated in the mornings and I'm like noooo! Not again, I took a pregnancy test and wouldn't you know, yep, pregnant.

I remember calling him, I said, "We have a problem," he asked me, "What do you want to do?" My mind was fixed. I already had two children, one with autism which equated to an extra child and I definitely couldn't afford another. So we did the "grown-up thing," Yep, you guessed, correctly, I scheduled an appointment to have an abortion. I was terrified. I felt conflicted, not convicted; there is a difference. I felt ashamed, so I reached out to my aunt. I told her what happened and she gave me some wisdom. Yes, we proceeded with the abortion; neither one of us wanted to have more kids. I had no idea where this relationship was going and I just didn't want to bring another child into this world and I didn't want to take the chance of having another child with autism.

Attitude adjustment

After the abortion, I found out that he was cheating on me, so I was done. I just stopped reaching out and responding to his calls. I decided I needed to get focused and started to pull back from dating. I focused on my sons and finding a career. I thought about going back to school for nursing again; but after working as a medical assistant, I knew that becoming a nurse wasn't for me.

There was an ultrasound tech in our office I noticed that she didn't have to be as hands on with the patients or the doctors. I thought to myself, I need that kind of job. I had been at the doctor's office for four years. One of the other medical assistants came in talking about going to a school in downtown Chicago for ultrasound, so we decided that we do it together.

We did our research only to find out that there was no financial aid and that we would need a co-signer for a student loan. I had no-one. There was a new African doctor in our office who took a liking to the other medical assistant. One day while we were all sitting around talking, we mentioned about going back to school and having difficulty finding someone to co-sign for our student loans. He volunteered to sign for us if we couldn't find anyone else. I didn't take him seriously at that time, but when I couldn't find anyone else, I prayed about it and then I approached him. He was shocked that I asked him, but he agreed to co-sign for me. I thanked him and I went into the bathroom, crying and praising God. I knew that going to school was going to change my life. I brought the paperwork to him. I was praying under my breath that he didn't changed his mind and he didn't. *He signed the papers for me and I was enrolled into ultrasound school!*

I just needed a babysitter. I reached out to my cousin who had just had a baby, I paid her to keep my boys on Saturdays while I caught the train to Chicago. Things were looking up. I was excited about having a new career so that I could take care of my sons. In the meantime, I continued going to church. We were going every Sunday and Wednesday. They had a healing and deliverance service. I had never heard of that before; but I began to heal. I remember just weeping in the worship services. All the pain, all the hurt, all the betrayal; all the things I had done, the fornicating, the abortions, I began to cry out for forgiveness. I would get so engulfed into the worship, it was like medicine to my soul. I would be at home worshipping God. My aunt and I would get up in the mornings to pray together, I was all in.

School was going well. Around my birthday, I got an email from my ex. We emailed back and forth. He tried to say that I misunderstood, blah, blah, blah. I told him we could be friends, but nothing more. I was focused on my relationship with God, going to school, and buying a house for me and my sons.

Then I got a call from the school about my loan. I didn't realize that there were two distributions dates, one at the beginning and then the next was at the six month mark. I had to get the doctor to sign the papers again. By the time of the six month distribution, this doctor was acting funny and he refused to co-sign for the next distribution. I was devastated. Everything was going so well, but I wasn't going to be able to finish school. I called my ex on the phone crying and he said, "Get the papers and I'll co-sign for you." Wait, what you're going to co-sign for me to go to school?" He said, "Yes" and he did. After that we were back together. No one had ever done anything like that for me. I thought that this meant we were supposed to be together. I fell back into that same pattern. I just couldn't break free from this cycle and he hadn't changed. Soon we were broken up, again.

My sons watched all of this play out. I wasn't even focused on them. They were well taken care of physically, but I was selfishly trying to fill a void inside of myself. I was so consumed with getting my needs met, that I didn't realize that I was following the generational patterns. I had to repent and I asked my sons for forgiveness, as well.

God was and is the only one who can heal and fill those places that needed and craved attention.

I finished school. I started looking for a new job so that I could get enough experience to take my exam and to get registered. No doors were opening up for me. I prayed, I asked God for direction and he answered. I went to my boss. I was so nervous to talk to him, but I pressed through. I knew that he was a progressive cardiologist who wanted to do more vascular ultrasound in his office. I told him that I had just graduated from ultrasound school and that I wanted to continue working for him. If he hired me as his vascular ultrasound tech, he could do more testing in his office. He paused, he put his finger on his chin in deep thought like a light bulb had come on. He accepted my offer. I told him that I needed more hands-on training, but I believe I could be up to par in a few months. He gave me a raise and eventually I was able to pass my registry exam, which gave me power to get another raise.

God has been so faithful to me. As I look back over my life, I can see the hand of God in every step. God was there playing an intricate role in the background while I was living my life. I'm sure you will see this as well.

I was doing what was natural. I was following the generational patterns and inflicting pain on myself. I had never completely healed from being sexually abused. I never healed from being beat up, the rejection, or the betrayal. I went through periods of depression, but I never sought help. Abortion after abortion, I had never even stopped to heal. I was numb. I couldn't feel anymore.

I did what most of us have been taught to do, we just keep moving forward, never pausing to heal our secret wounds.

My story is my story, it's my truth and it may not be the worst you've ever heard or it maybe it is. The point is, I didn't tell my story to get sympathy or to offend anyone or to feel shame all over again. I'm telling my truth to show you a pattern of how wounds are formed, starting in early childhood. I'm telling my story so that one day you will tell your truth.

This is not my complete story, of course. For the most part, as you read my story you can see that there is a pattern that I kept falling into; abuse, hurt, rejection, deception, depression over and over again.

I had to make the decision to stop, to really get focused on my children and heal. I asked God to teach me how to be a mother and to heal me from my past.

I am not ashamed of my past because everything that I have been through and all the pain that I've caused myself have been forgiven. God knew and knows my story. Nothing that has happened has caught Him by surprise. I have forgiven everyone that has ever hurt me and I have forgiven myself, as well.

There is freedom in telling your truth, I am free from condemnation, guilt and shame. My desire is for all of you to be free and that is the desire of our Heavenly Father, as well.

Healing is a journey. It will not happen overnight. It may take years to truly feel free; but it's a journey worth taking. Your healing is your responsibility, even if you're not responsible for how you got your wounds.

Take the time to write your story; allow God to heal you from the inside out and then allow God to give purpose to your pain.

CHAPTER 3

"WILL YOU BE MADE WHOLE?"

What's your story? We all have one. As you could see in my story, there were things that happened to me (sins committed by another person against me) and things I caused myself (my personal sins). This is not to place blame, shame or guilt. These are the tactics that the devil uses to keep our focus off of healing. It is more important to identify the soul wound and how it is affecting us, so that we can be healed.

We all have unresolved feelings that we have harbored in our hearts against people in our present and/or past relationships, because we felt that we were treated unfairly. Every human being at some point or another has experienced unfairness.

Rejection and abandonment are two of the most common soul wounds. We all have experienced rejection; whether it was from a child on the playground who didn't want to play with us or not being picked to play dodge ball. Rejection is defined as the act of pushing something or someone away; refusing to accept or withhold love from. This can be experienced on a large scale or in a small way in everyday life. Rejection is very hurtful.

An example of this would be:

When a child is abandoned by a parent, which is a very traumatic experience. That trauma creates a seed of rejection that is planted into that child's heart, which creates a soul wound. These wounds attach to our soul toppled with other life events to create a stronghold of fear and rejection. All of these things shape us into the people that we are. As we can see from the present state of our world, there is a desperate need for restoration in our souls.

"Hurting people do hurt other people," this is such a true statement that we just can't ignore. Our hurts, grievances, misunderstandings and mistreatments, compiled with our inability as a society to resolve conflicts has fueled anger, rage and hate. These issues have caused us to be unforgiving and unable to reconcile our differences. This leads to divorce, division in families, broken relationships; in extreme cases suicide, murder, racism and terrorism.

"For it is from within, out of a person's heart, that evil thoughts come; sexual immorality, theft, murder, adultery, greed, malice, deceit, lewdness, envy, slander, arrogance and folly. All these evils come from the inside and defile a person." Mark 7: 21-23 (NKJV)

Why do I bring these issues up? These are all wounds in our soul and ways that we act out as a results of our soul's condition. When something horrific happens, the first question people tend to ask is, "What is wrong with this world?" The answer is it's a heart problem, it's a lack of love for oneself and a lack of love for other people. The Bible says, "To love your neighbor as yourself". Unfortunately, we do not have a real understanding about what love is or how to demonstrate it. The world's view of love is based on conditions (if you love me, then I will love you). But the Bible says, "Do to others as you would have them do to you. If you love those who love you, what credit is that to you. Even sinners love those who love them." Luke 6:31-32 (NIV)

Unfortunately, most of us are in an "emotional intensive care," due to the high expectations that we impose on people. There is this assumption that some person is supposed to be our "everything" and will supply all of our physical and emotional needs. This is unrealistic. I'm guilty! This causes disappointment, frustration and anger which lead to strife. The truth is that no one has the ability to live up to our expectations, except Jesus.

Due to this mindset we have a whole lot of people walking around like ticking time bombs because of unmet "needs." These issues can stem from our present relationships or a childhood experience when we didn't get affirmations from a parent. Whatever the case, these things cause wounds to our soul.

I had to learn the hard way, that there is no person on this earth who has everything that I need. There is no one who has the capacity to love me the way that I need to be loved. It is only through the unconditional love of Jesus Christ that we can know and receive love. And it is Christ's love that can heal and change our hearts.

We are in dire need of inner healing and deliverance. We are in need of unconditional love. Praise be to God that we have a Great Physician who is the lover of our souls, Jesus. He is the only one who can heal our wounds.

We must want healing. Healing our soul is a personal journey that we must desire. No other person can access healing for you or me. Without proper healing, our pain and hurt will seep out into the way we think, into our interactions with people, and into our reactions to life's circumstances. It affects how we treat people, inevitably it affects how we think and feel about ourselves.

There is healing for your soul but do you want it?

Jesus boldly asked this question to the man lying in an invalid state by a pool for 38 years. Can you imagine, just lying there, suffering?

"Sometime later, Jesus went to Jerusalem for one of the Jewish festivals. Now there is in Jerusalem near the Sheep Gate a pool called Bethesda. Here a great number of disabled people used to lie; the blind, the lame, the paralyzed. For an angel went down at a certain season into the pool, and troubled the water; who ever got in first after the troubling of the water was made whole of whatever disease he had. One who was there had been an

invalid for thirty-eight years. When Jesus saw him lying there and learned that he had been in this condition for a long time, he asked him, "Do you want to be get well?" John 5:1-6 (NIV)

Jesus blatantly asked him, "Do you want to be made whole?" The man's response is:

"Sir, I have no one to help me into the pool when the water is stirred. While I am trying to get in, someone else goes down ahead of me." John 5:7 (NIV)

I can understand why Jesus asked him this question. Surely after thirty-eight years of lying there, one would think of a strategy to get into the pool before everyone else, right? After being there that long, he would have known the exact time that the angel was going to come to stir the waters. At the very least, he could roll himself down to the edge of the pool to be ready, but he didn't.

Unfortunately, there are a lot people who do not want to be healed. They don't want divine help with their problems. They see their situation as a means of attention, sympathy and/or a "pity party". They crave the attention more than they want the healing. Then there are the proud. These are people who will never admit that they have weaknesses, hurts and pains. Absolutely nothing bothers them at all, they have an, 'I'm all good attitude', nothing hurts or bothers me. It's sad to say that inwardly we know the condition that we are in, but will refuse help due to our complacency or because of pride. Everyone needs healing. The person that denies it the most adamantly is usually the one that needs it the most. These people have put themselves in a self-protection mode where walls have been built up to protect them from outside influences. Sadly what happens is no-one is allowed in and they can't get out either; a self- imposed prison has been constructed.

What hinders healing?

Denial and unforgiveness are the biggest hindrances to healing. Denial is our first defense mechanism against change. We use it to protect ourselves, to look tough or like we have it all together. Honesty with ourselves is the first step in healing. When we can admit that we are wounded to ourselves, then and only then can we seek help. Unforgiveness hinders the progression of our healing because it keeps us in bondage (more in chapter 5). Denial will only prolong and hinder us from getting the healing that our soul is crying out for.

Are you sitting in denial? Are you waiting for someone to come along to help you get healed? Are you sitting back complaining?

The story about the ten lepers shows us how we ought to seek help. These men had heard about Jesus's healing ministry but due to their illness they were banished to live outside of the city limits in isolation. When they saw Jesus they called out for mercy and received their healing in the process. They didn't deny their condition and they weren't too proud to embarrass themselves for the sake of their need. They wanted their healing and they received it.

It's very easy to complain and even justify our wounds because they are real. Abuse is real, rejection is real, and divorce is real. Any of the hurtful situations that we have been through and will face in this life are justifiable, but we shouldn't stay camped there. When you decide to stay wounded, your wounds will affect how you make decisions for your life. Instead of reacting from a logical place, you will react out of your feelings. Those wounded places become strongholds where you will inadvertently allow the devil to come in to control you.

Unhealed wounds leave you open to all kinds of attacks from the enemy. Guilt, bitterness, anger, doubt, unforgiveness are all self-imposed prisons that are used as forms of protection, but they hinder you from moving forward in life and will cause you to act out of your true character.

Unhealed wounds in your soul can cause you to make irrational decisions. Unhealed wounds will cause you to have a wrong outlook on life which will cause you to bend the truth and operate out of anger, rage, unforgiveness and in an unloving way.

I'll use my life as an example.

After being abused, misused, rejected, beat-up, betrayed and cheated on, I was angry, hurt and broken. I decided in my heart that no one was ever going to hurt me again. My motto was, "I'll hurt you before you hurt me," meaning I'll reject you before you reject me. This never works because we are human. We are made to have intimacy and relationships. So, gradually I would let my walls down, to let someone come close to my heart, and of course, just like any other time I would get hurt.

I was subconsciously trying to find someone to complete me, someone to come in to take care of my heart. I was looking for someone to make me feel valued, special and important. I wanted to be wanted. But because of my brokenness I kept attracting the same type of people with different degrees of brokenness. You will attract who you are on the inside, which can be very toxic, and dysfunctional, if you have a wounded soul.

Jesus came to give us life and life more abundantly. That word abundantly means plentiful and overflowing. He did not come so that we could live a mediocre and depressed life, filled with lack. He desires that we would be whole and that we would have everything that we need to fulfill our purpose.

Will you be made whole?

If your answer is yes, ask the Lord to heal your soul. You can pray a simple prayer asking God to heal your soul like David did in Psalms 41:4 (NASB)

As for me, "O Lord, be gracious to me; Heal my soul, for I have sinned against You."

As we move forward, please be advised that this journey to healing your soul wounds will take your cooperation, commitment and partnership with God; God will not go against your will. He will not force Himself upon you, but He is committed to helping us through this journey.

CHAPTER 4

UNCOVERING YOUR WOUNDS

When I was a little girl I was a "tomboy," I played rough with the boys. I liked climbing trees and fences. My brothers and I would race each other up and down the street, barefoot. I can remember falling off or being flipped off my bike, skinning up my knees, plenty of times. I wasn't concerned about having scars because it just came with the territory, besides we were having fun. Most of those wounds are gone now, but I still can see a few if I look closely at my legs and elbows today. Luckily, I never broke any bones or had any major accidents or hospital stays. My older brother on the other hand has had a few close calls. I remember my mother had to leave to take care of business. We were to stay inside the apartment. We decided to chase each other.

Somehow my brother ended up standing on the kitchen counter; he accidently knocked over a glass jar, it shattered all over the floor. Before we knew it, he jumped down off of the counter landing on a large piece of glass that went into his foot. Blood was everywhere; it was horrible. He had to have a lot of stitches. They also gave him crutches, because he couldn't put pressure on that foot, to avoid breaking open his stitches.

This wound was in a vulnerable place and limited him from being able to function independently, for a while. It was a deep wound that was very slow to heal, but eventually it did. God has made our bodies in an amazing way. Our bodies typically heal on their own, unless the wound is too deep that it needs intervention.

Most of our scrapes, bruises, paper cuts are surface wounds that just automatically heal on their own without any assistance. With the exception of paper cuts, we may not experience a whole lot of pain, with these types of wounds.

Deeper wounds, such as lacerations and puncture wounds may require a little more tender care; such as peroxide, Neosporin and maybe even stitches. These type of wounds are even more painful than surface wounds. The deeper the wound, the more attention the wound requires, for example a stab wound or a gunshot wound will require further examination. The deeper the wound the more vulnerable your vital organs are. The deeper the wound, the higher the risk of infection.

Deeper wounds require more specialized and immediate care because we can't see inside the body with the naked eye. If someone falls from a three story building, they may have internal bleeding and/or a head injury, right? Most people who are involved in a major accident typically need emergency care just to make sure that they don't have internal bleeding or other internal injuries.

Well, our soul wounds require that same type of attention. Soul wounds are harder to detect, unlike our physical wounds. Soul wounds are invisible, they are more difficult to see and diagnosis. Soul wounds are deep wounds.

On this journey of uncovering our secret wounds, we must acknowledge that the wounds are there; we must pull off the bandages, so that the wounds can be exposed to the air and light.

We do this with our physical wounds all the time. Because we can't see our soul wounds we leave bandages on for far too long, which hinders the wound from healing properly. Leaving a bandage on for too long can slow the healing process and becomes a breeding ground for infection. Infections affect everything and left untreated can lead to disability and even death.

To uncover something means to remove the cover from and expose it; to find or become aware of what was hidden; to be seen by removing the cover.

What is a soul?

Our soul is the most valuable thing that we have in our possession; it is referenced in the Bible over 400 times. Here's an example:

Now may the God of peace Himself sanctify you entirely; and may your spirit and soul and body be preserved complete, without blame at the coming of the Lord Jesus Christ. 1 Thessalonians 5:23 (NIV)

We are a three part being, according to 1 Thessalonians 5:23; spirit, soul and body. Our soul comprises our mind, will and emotions which controls our conscience, intellect, personality and desires. Our soul is where we choose whether our spirit will serve God (works of the spirit) or the devil (works of the flesh). Our soul and spirit are our eternal components that continue on into eternity after our physical bodies die. Our soul and spirit live on.

Biblically speaking, our soul would be referenced as our "heart or mind." The Greek word for "heart" is kardia, it's the emotional center of our being, and the capacity of moral preference. It is the part of us that produces desire and makes us who we are. It is the inner part of our minds where decisions are made.

We have a physical heart that pumps our blood and we have a spiritual heart (mind) where God examines our intentions.

Every man's way is right in his own eyes, but the Lord weighs the heart. Proverbs 21:2 (NASB)

Jeremiah 17:10 (NASB) says, "I, the Lord, search the heart and test the mind, even to give to each man according to his ways, according to the results of his deeds.

A soul wound is an emotional hurt, pain or trauma that that has not been properly addressed. Yes, especially those wounds from childhood. Childhood wounds can still have a negative effect on our life. Childhood is such a large part of our life. It is where the foundation of who we are is formed: our morals, our first relationships with people, our understanding about how we should be treated and how we are to treat others. Our self-worth is established in childhood. This is where we learn how to cope with our frustrations, hurts, and pain.

We mimic the people who are closes to us, i.e. parents and siblings. And if these relationships have unhealthy coping mechanisms, they can sabotage the rest of our lives. It is important to understand, that soul wounds don't start in adulthood, they start in childhood.

Example:

When a child witnesses domestic violence, they react as though it were happening to them. They have a fear of harm or abandonment, excessive worry, anger issues, guilt, emotional distancing and poor judgment.

Soul wounds do affect us and it so important to uncover these wounds so that healing can take place.

The root cause of a soul wound can be:

- Physical, mental and verbal abuse

- Emotional abuse (withholding love and affection can be inflicted by a spouse or parent) ~ (not feeling good enough or loved enough)

- Ungodly soul ties (soulish connections made between two or more people; developed through intercourse and agreements)

- Traumas – (sexual abuse child molestation, human sex trafficking; kidnapping, rape etc.)

- Broken relationships – (family rejection, favoritism, divorce, adultery)

- Generational curses – (patterns of behaviors that can be seen in each generation- domestic violence, abuse, alcoholism, poverty, incarceration are a few examples)

- Abandonment – (orphaned, divorce, death, suicide, addiction; feeling unwanted)

- Rejection – (not being accepted or acknowledged by children, adults or in families)

- Bullying - (harassment and gossiping)

- Acts of violence – (drive by shootings, mass shootings, acts of terrorism; school shootings; violent attacks, robberies, being held hostage or against your will)

All of these things mentioned above attach to our souls and plant seeds in our heart. Maybe you aren't sure how you may be affected by your wounds; here are some behaviors that are the fruit of the seeds planted by soul wounds.

- No confidence - low self-esteem (loss of your voice)

- Needy or clingy (the fear of being alone-loneliness)

- Anger, bitterness, hate and violence (short tempered and violent behavior)

- Fear of people, fear of failure and fear of success

- Shame, guilt and unworthiness

- Self-condemnation and self-hate

- Lonely and withdrawn

- Social anxiety
- Arrested psychological development - (stagnation; being stuck in an emotional level of development)
- Rejection - (unable to give nor receive love; unable to respond to others properly)
- Promiscuity - (seeking love and attention)
- Eating disorders - (anorexia, bulimia, gluttony)
- Suicide and Suicidal tendencies
- Abusive behavior - (you start hurting people the way you were hurt)
- Self-mutilation - (cutting)
- Post-Traumatic Stress Syndrome – PTSD (usually happens after a traumatic or terrifying event; with triggers that can bring back memories of the trauma accompanied by intense emotional and physical reactions.

These behaviors are red flags, which tell us that something is wrong. Instead of addressing these red flags, we embrace these behaviors as a part of our personality.

These behaviors are the fruit of our soul wounds, they are not a part of our personality. We must identify the root cause of the behavior. Instead, we try to modify our behavior without identifying the root cause of the behavior, which is a temporary fix.

A good example of this is, pulling weeds out of a garden, if we only pull the weed that is on the surface without the root, that weed will keep coming back.

We must take action by digging deep (self-examination), identify the root (make a list), pull the root out (submit this to God), so that we can heal well.

We must uncover the secret wounds that have hindered us from healing, being whole, living in peace and being authentic with ourselves.

The Bible says, in Proverbs 18:14 (NASB) that we can't bear or handle a wounded spirit. This scripture tells us that it is easier to suffer with a physical wound than to attempt to deal with a wounded spirit. This is why we must partner with God for our healing.

As stated previously, our secret wounds need the same attention or more than our physical wounds need.

Now, the work begins.

CHAPTER 5

HEALING WELL

I love the story in the Bible about the prodigal son's return home to his father. This young man thought he had what it took to survive without his father. However, he learned very quickly how much he didn't know and how much he truly needed his father. In this story, the father freely gives him his inheritance (free will), so that he could go out into the world on his own. He quickly squanders the gifts he was given and finds himself broken and in need of help. He hires himself out to make ends meet. He finds himself feeding pigs and longing to eat the pigs' foods.

He had hit rock bottom, physically, mentally, emotionally and morally.

I love the verse where it says, "He came to himself," Luke 15:17 (KJV). He came to his senses; his reality set in; he woke up.

Before we can be restored with God, we must wake up and see where we are and how bad that we are; we must come to the end of ourselves and our abilities.

As he walked along, he rehearsed what he was going to say to his father; how he would repent and humble himself even to the point of being one of his father's hired help. Unbeknownst to him, his father had been looking and waiting for his son to come back home. While he was still a long way off, his father saw him and was filled with compassion for him; he ran to his son, threw his arms around him and kissed his neck. Luke 15:20 (NASB)

Now, this young man had been working in the heat of the day, in the mud, slinging pig dung and sleeping with the pigs. He was filthy and stinky, but his father did not hesitate to run to him, embrace him and kiss him on his neck. Then he had his servants bring the best robe, a ring for his finger and sandals for his feet and proceeded to throw a feast for his son who was lost, but now found.

This father did not wait until the son was all cleaned up, he did not wait until his son went to get himself “together”, but this father welcomed his son back and kissed his son on the neck. A kiss on the neck denotes an intimate relationship, not in the way of a man kisses a woman or vice versa but it showed the extent of this father’s love for his son. The Father’s love never ends, there are no conditions on it and there is nothing a child can do to lose the love of the Father.

This parable gives us an amazing picture of how our Heavenly Father sees us and how he longs for our return to Him. He doesn’t wait until we are all cleaned up or until we have it all together. He stands waiting with open arms while we are stinky, dirty and sinking in sin. He loves us so much that even while we were yet sinners, He sent His only son to save us. He loves us with an everlasting love; it never ends.

“I have loved you with an everlasting love; I have drawn you with unfailing kindness.” Jeremiah 31:3 (NIV)

Our Father God, is the lover of our souls and he is the only who can heal us. We can go to the doctor for treatment. We can go to therapy for management, but God our Father is the only one who can heal us. Healing only comes from Him.

"I will restore you to health and heal your wounds, "declares the Lord." Jeremiah 30:17 (NASB)

"I am the Lord who heals you." Exodus 15:26 (NASB)

How do we heal well?

Acknowledging the truth about yourself

The first step in healing is acknowledging that there is a problem and that we need help. We must stop lying to ourselves and be completely honest with ourselves.

The first step for a new member of Alcoholics Anonymous is admitting that they are powerless over alcohol and that their lives have become unmanageable. The first step to healing is admitting that we are powerless and that we need a Savior. Just like the prodigal son, we must come to ourselves. We can blame others and we can pretend that all is well, ignoring what's happening on the inside or we can STOP.

We must stop to examine ourselves. We must stop to feel; we must stop to see our internal condition. The prodigal son paused to look at his environment. He saw how far he had fallen. He saw how his condition had changed so drastically from his father's house to a pig pen. It was not a pretty picture. He stopped to do a self-check. He had to repent and ask for forgiveness. How many of us are carrying around a pig pen in our soul? I'm guilty! I, too, had to stop to do a self-check and repent. I had to ask myself some hard questions:

Why have I allowed this abuse? Why am I so angry? Why does this keep happening to me?

I had to check my heart's motives. I asked God to search my heart to reveal any fear, unforgiveness or bitterness and any areas where I was still broken.

I implore you to ask yourself the hard questions. If you can't be real with yourself, who can you be real with?

Repentance

I had to repent because I had people and things in my heart where only God should reside. No one should have total access to your whole heart. The Bible says, "To love the Lord your God with ALL your heart, all your soul and all your mind." God has to be Lord over your heart, soul and mind. Otherwise we get damaged by people, who do try to love us but don't know how to love us, effectively.

When we give people and things access to our whole heart, we make them an idol and put them in a position where they are able to manipulate and hurt us. Now, don't get me wrong, most people are not out here trying to hurt people intentionally. Because we all have been wounded in some type of way, it happens. We are human and we mimic what we see. We have learned behaviors from family and friends that just may not be healthy. Most of the time, we really don't know that it's an unhealthy behavior pattern until someone comes along and tells us.

It takes humility to see the error in our ways and want to correct it.

For all have sinned and fall short of the glory of God Romans 3:23 (NASB)

Repentance makes us at peace with God; it also brings a refreshing, restoration and healing. When we repent, turning from our sinful nature, the devil has no legal rights to bring back up that sin, because it's covered under the blood of Jesus.

Therefore, repent and return, so that your sins may be wiped away, in order that times of refreshing may come from the presence of the Lord. Acts 3:9 (NASB)

Here is a sample repentance prayer that you should pray out loud

Father God, Lord Jesus,

"I am a sinner, and I ask for your forgiveness. Lord, forgive me for allowing people and things to become idols in my heart. Forgive me for allowing these things and people to occupy the space in my heart that is only carved out for you. Father, I ask you to cleanse me from all unrighteousness, as I submit my heart to you. I accept Jesus as my Lord and Savior, in the name of Jesus.

Amen.

Forgiveness

This step is so vital to healing your wounds because your soul is not the only thing that is at stake, your health is also dependent on it.

Holding a grudge, being disgruntled and angry only hurts you; it makes you resentful and bitter. Anger, resentment and bitterness are now being linked to cardiovascular diseases, such as heart disease, strokes and high blood pressure. Forgiveness is an act of spiritual, emotional and physical healing.

Forgiveness is never for the other person, but it's for you. Forgiveness isn't based upon how worthy we are. It's a gift that is given out of mercy. We must understand that if we don't forgive those who have hurt us, then our Father in heaven will not forgive us.

Unforgiveness is a sin; it hinders our prayers, hardens our hearts, places us in spiritual bondage and it means there is an eternal separation from God. I don't know about you, but there is no one worth going to hell for.

Forgiveness does not mean restoration or reconciliation. Forgiveness does not depend upon whether the offender has apologized or not. You may never get an apology and you have to be okay with that. It's tight but it's right.

I understand that it is really hard to forgive those who have caused us pain and it feels unfair to release them, even while you're still suffering. My beloved, don't take revenge, but leave that to the righteous anger of God, for it is written, "Vengeance is mine, I will repay." (Romans 12:19 NKJV) God our Father can pay back wrong better than we ever could, but we must be willing to release them to Him, so that He can do what only He can do. If we try to take control of the situation by seeking revenge, then God has no obligation to deal with that person; and we end up making things worse for ourselves.

We must forgive so that we can move forward and trust that God will handle the rest. God is faithful to bless us because of our obedience to Him.

Forgiving yourself

We must forgive ourselves for the things we have done or allowed in our lives. This step always slips by. There are people who are filled with guilt and shame for things they have done or had no control over. We all have sinned and fall short of the glory of God, constantly. This will not change until we are in heaven. Free yourself from this self-imposed prison cell and know that God is faithful and just to forgive us of all sin and cleanse us of all unrighteousness.

We find peace and freedom in the finished works of Jesus on the cross. When we punish ourselves, we crucify Him afresh. Jesus suffered once and for all. He was wounded for our transgressions, bruised for our iniquities; the chastisement of our peace was upon Him and by His strips we are healed. Isaiah 53:5 (NKJV)

Jesus Christ suffered the punishment for our sins so we could experience forgiveness and peace. Embrace His forgiveness and peace today.

We should always examine ourselves to ensure that we are not operating in unforgiveness and/or being unforgiving towards ourselves. Ask the Lord to forgive you and ask Him to help you set your heart to forgive automatically. Examine yourself daily to protect yourself from this sin.

Seeing your worth

When we examine ourselves, it's not so that we can point out our sins, our mistakes and certainly not our failures. We examine ourselves to see our worth. God wants us to see our value, how much he has deposited into us. He wants us to see our potential, to bring light into a dark and dying world; our potential to love and live a life that is poured out for Him. He wants us to live life and have it more abundantly.

Our potential is only found in the One who created us, God, our Father. He is the potter and we are the clay and all of us are the work of His hands. Outside of God, our Father, we can do nothing. This is why our personal relationship with Father God is so vital to our healing and our ability to heal well.

Ephesians 1:11-12 (MSG)

It's in Christ that we find out who we are and what we are living for. Long before we first heard of Christ and got our hopes up, he had his eye on us, had designs in us for glorious living, part of the overall purpose he is working out in everything and everyone.

Ephesians 1:4-5 (NLT)

Even before He made the world, God loved us and chose us in Christ to be holy and without fault in His eyes. God decided in advance to adopt us into His own family by bring us to Himself through Jesus Christ. This is what He wanted to do, and it gave Him great pleasure.

This scripture show us that we were not an afterthought, but a forethought, meaning, He thought of us when He created the heavens and the earth and the fullness thereof. There are many people walking around, thinking that God is mad at them or that he made a mistake when he created them. But it's not true. You were wanted from the beginning.

He loves us. He chose us. He made us without fault and He made us holy. He adopted us so that we could be a part of His family and he took great pleasure in doing these things for us.

We must see ourselves how God sees us; he sees us as a necessity not an accessory.

God took great care when He created us. We are His prized possessions. We must understand how valuable we are and that the most valuable possession that we have is our soul.

Mark 8:36 (NASB) says, "For what does it profit a man, to gain the whole world and forfeit his soul."

Even if we possessed all the expensive things in the world: the biggest mansion, the most expensive cars and even if you were the wealthiest person in the world, it still would pale in comparison to the value of your soul.

Remember we are a three part being: spirit, soul and body. When we get saved, we automatically get a new spirit, however our soul remains the same. Our soul is too valuable for God to replace, it contains our personality, our DNA, our gifts and talents. It contains our unique make up that makes us into individual people for God's purposes. We must partner with God to renew our souls by allowing God's love to overshadow all the hurt and disappointments and by allowing the word of God to transform us. When we come to know of the word and believe God's love for us, our soul is renewed.

We must understand the value of our soul and how to take care of it. This is why healing our soul wounds is so important and a very intentional process. A wounded soul hinders us from discovering who we truly are in Christ, which doesn't allow us to live an abundant life of peace, joy and freedom.

Seek godly counsel

Sitting down with someone to help unpack our past issues so that we can discover a clear path to our future is so necessary and valuable. A lot of people think that counseling is taboo or something you only do if you have mental health issues, but this is not true. The truth is that we all have mental health issues but some are more severe than others. Ignoring them will not help us. The more we ignore these past hurts, the more power and authority we give these issues to take over and infect everything in our lives.

Let's dispel this lie about counseling. Counseling doesn't mean that something is wrong. It is getting wisdom and a different perspective on a subject matter that we are struggling with. Counseling is getting new tools in our tool belts, to help us make the right decisions for our life.

This negative attitude or mindset about counseling is a stronghold called "pride". Healing requires humility and vulnerability. Don't allow pride to rob you of your healing.

Proverbs 19:20 (NASB) says, “Listen to counsel and accept discipline, that you may be wise the rest of your life.” Seeking godly counsel has so many benefits and it is biblically sound. It gives us another set of eyes and ears and gives us time to think of options to consider. Sometimes we just don’t know what the next step should be or maybe we are looking at the current life issue with the wrong attitude. So having another person to bounce things off of is so beneficial.

It is so important to find the right person to counsel you. I would not recommend receiving counsel from someone who is in a worse condition then you are. I would also say do not accept counsel from the unwise. Psalms 1:1 (NKJV) says, “Not to seek counsel from the ungodly. I would say no to family and/or friends because it will limit your ability to be open and honest.

Pray for God’s guidance in finding the right person. When we step in faith and ask God to lead us to the right person, we must be careful not to look at the outward appearance: socioeconomic status, racial or cultural background. Whether the person has this degree or that degree is irrelevant. These are the world’s standards of finding a counselor not God’s. God sees the heart. He isn’t impressed by the outward appearance or status. God will send someone who is seasoned and wise, who can relate to your background and who has the time and patience to devote to you and your needs.

Here are some necessary characteristics of a godly counselor:

- **Wisdom -** a good counselor applies knowledge of God's word to their lives every day, in their interactions with family, friends and strangers. Proverbs 10:14 (NIV) says, "Wise men store up knowledge, but fools invite ruin.

- **Discernment** - a good counselor will have discernment so that they may know and approve the things that are excellent, in order to be sincere and blameless. Their lives are submitted to prayer, to scripture and leading from the Holy Spirit.

  And this is my prayer: that your love may abound more and more in knowledge and depth of insight, so that you may be able to discern what is best and may be pure and blameless for the day of Christ, filled with the fruit of righteousness that comes through Jesus Christ. Philippians 1:9-10 (NIV)

- **Knowledge -** a good counselor is well acquainted with sound teaching from the word of God. They are people who stick to the solid truths of God's word and are discerning.

- **Truthfulness -** a good counselor will speak the hard truth to you in love. They want you to live righteously and not be ignorant.

  Instead, speaking the truth in love, we grow to become in every respect the mature body of him who is the head that is Christ. Ephesians 4:15 (NIV)

- **Integrity** - a good counselor strives to live a life of integrity. The testimony of their conscience is in holiness, godly sincerity and trust. Your personal information is trusted in good hands.

Now this is our boast: Our conscience testifies that we have conducted ourselves in the world, and especially in our relations with you, with integrity and godly sincerity. We have done so, relying not on worldly wisdom but on God's grace.

2 Corinthians 1:12 (NIV)

These are a few things I look for in a counselor but also in anyone who is to be in my close inner circle. These qualities create a secure atmosphere for healing and growth to take place. Please choose wisely.

In the next chapter, we will continue on our journey to healing our soul's wounds by taking practical steps to ensure we heal well.

CHAPTER 6

BE TRANSFORMED BY THE RENEWING OF YOUR MIND

And do not be conformed to this world, but be transformed by the renewing of your mind, so that you may prove what the will of God is, that which is good and acceptable and perfect. Romans 12:2 (NASB)

As we uncover our wounds, we must allow Father God to thoroughly clean us. It is a process to rid the body of substances regarded as toxic or unhealthy by typically consuming water. Some synonyms for cleanse are; to bathe, to disinfect, to purify or to wash.

1 John 1:9 (NIV) says, “If we confess our sins, he is faithful and just to forgive us our sins and to cleanse us from all unrighteousness.

I love the definition of cleanse. It first tells us that cleansing is a thorough process, which means this process will take deep thought and complete regard to every detail.

Then we must get rid of toxic and unhealthy substances in our minds by the washing of the word of God. We must remove negative people, things, thinking and habits and replace these with the word of God.

Are you ready? If so keep reading.

Our battlefield is not with anything physical but it is a spiritual battle played out on the battlefield of our minds. Our fight to healing our soul wounds has to do with our heart or mind. Remember that our soul is referenced as our heart or mind. It is our mind, will, emotions, intellect and imagination. Our soul is the emotional center of our being. It is the inner part of our minds where decisions are made.

“For the weapons of our warfare are not carnal, but mighty through God to the pulling down of strongholds.” 2 Corinthians 10:4 (NKJV)

A stronghold is an incorrect thinking pattern that has molded itself into our way of thinking. It's referred to as a fortress which is difficult to access. It is a place where a particular cause or belief is strongly defended or upheld.

The term stronghold is described as mindset or an attitude. These attitudes and mindsets can be lies which we have allowed to distort or confuse our thinking; a lie that has gained a foothold in our mind or emotions and then our behavior. These lies are seeds that produce fruit which distort the way we see and think. This fruit will affect our faith and interfere with our ability to possess the truths of the gospel.

Proverbs 23:7 (KJV) says, "As a man thinketh in his heart so is he, meaning our thoughts govern our lives, we become what we think about. You are where you are today because of your thoughts and you will be tomorrow where your thoughts take you.

Strongholds have the capacity to affect our feelings, how we respond to situations in life and they play a huge role in our spiritual freedom. The foundation of strongholds is deception and lies. They are built from a wide variety of sources, including our environment, our parents, the people around us and evil spirits.

Why are we talking about strongholds? Strongholds are constructed in our lives by a wound, experience, or disappointment that makes our heart ripe for lies to be planted. The enemy uses our fears, our wants and our secrets against us, to build strongholds. The enemy then begins to build a wall of lies and inaccurate ideas about who God is. These lies opens the door for misinterpretation of the word of God. This can cause us to have prideful thoughts and distorted views about how God sees us, especially when we sin.

We cannot believe the lies of the enemy, these lies are partial truths with no solid evidence. The enemy has no power over us, all he can do is present an idea to us. It's when we come into agreement with these lies that they become strongholds, which the enemy fiercely defends so that he can continue to control us.

Strongholds have a reoccurring pattern. They have a "strong-grip" on us, which makes it hard to break free from them and we find ourselves reverting back to certain behaviors. This cycle keeps happening until we renew our minds to think like God.

How do strongholds get established?

Strongholds are established when we have unconfessed and unrepentant sin in our lives. There is no sin that is greater than the cross. However God cannot heal what you will not confess or own up to. The enemy loves secrecy and will establish a stronghold in our unexposed sin.

Here are other areas where strongholds are established

- Unbelief (doubt about God's faithfulness)
- Shame and Condemnation
- Rejection – is a stronghold that opens the door to others (listed below); this stronghold goes against God's plan of family and community, by rejecting, isolating and intimidating every aspect of a person's life.
- Pride
- Anger
- Unforgiveness
- Rebellion/stubbornness
- Bitterness
- Depression
- Addiction

- Lies (Lies about God; lies about yourself and how God sees you)

- Occult activity (engaging in occult practices; psychics, fortune tellers, Wicca; mediums; dream catchers, crystals etc.)

- Generational curses (unhealthy and ungodly family traditions and family patterns passed down from generation to generation)

We must replace these negative mindsets and attitudes with the word of God.

He must become our stronghold, our refuge and our savior.

Let's continue,

Casting down imaginations and every high thing that exalts itself against the knowledge of God. 2 Corinthians 10:5 (NKJV)

Where we once allowed negative thoughts and thinking patterns to run amuck, now we must retrain our minds to think on good things, things that build us up; things of a good report. We must think like God thinks. We can no longer let what we think other people think about us rule. We can no longer accept negative childhood labels or low self-esteem to rule, but we must allow God's word which is alive and powerful and it is useful for teaching and training in righteousness to rule.

The mind governed by the flesh is death, but the mind governed by the Spirit is life and peace. Romans 8:6 (NKJV)

We must compare our thoughts with the word of God. We must identify the thoughts that fill our minds on a regular basis and compare what we are thinking to what God says. In order to do this, we must read the word of God, so that we will know when we are receiving something that is contrary to what God says, otherwise, we will continue to be bombarded with the lies of the enemy.

We must bring into captivity every thought to the obedience of Christ." 2 Corinthians 10:5 (NKJV)

Bringing every thought captive to the obedience of Christ will take a lot of intentionality and hard work, but you can do it!

So, if God's word says one thing and your mind is thinking the opposite, your thinking is wrong; not the word of God. God is true and every man is a liar. We do not have to believe lies anymore because we know the truth.

Here I'll give you an example:

The enemy of our souls loves to tell us that no one loves us, when actually God's word clearly tells us that in John 3:16 (NKJV), God so loved the world that he gave his only begotten Son. The word "world," in this verse is defined as "human race or mankind;" He loved you and I so much that he sacrificed His only son for us, now that's love. We have to debunk the lies that we have been taught with the truth of the word of God.

Here's another lie the enemy tries to use: You're a failure and you will never be good enough. We can destroy this lie with Philippians 4:13 (NKJV) "I can do all things through Christ who strengthens me," and Romans 8:37(NKJV) "I am more than a conquer through Him who loved me."

Jesus used this same strategy while being tempted in the wilderness; here let's read it.

"And the tempter came and said to Him, "if You are the Son of God, command that these stones become bread." But He answered and said, "it is written, man shall not live on bread alone, but on every word that proceeds out of the mouth of God." Then the devil took Him into the holy city and had Him stand on the pinnacle of the temple, and said to Him, "If You are the Son of God, throw Yourself down; for it is written, "He will command His angels concerning

You, and on their hands they will bear you up, so that you will not strike your foot against a stone." Matthew 4:3-6 (NASB)

Now, watch Jesus's response, *"On the other hand, it is written, 'You shall not put the Lord your God to the test." Matthew 4:7 (NASB)*

Jesus has given us an example of how we are to respond to the lies of the enemy and lies that we have been taught. He also shows us that we must thoroughly study the word of God so that we know when the word is being twisted to manipulate us.

When we know the word of God, we are able to rightly determine if what we are thinking is from God or another source. We are able to take every thought captive and make it obedient to Christ, so that we can demolish the strongholds that have had us in bondage. Then we will know the truth about ourselves.

The word of God washes us and transforms our minds so that we have the mind of Christ. When our minds are rooted in the word, then we will know the truth, and the truth will make us free." John 8:32 (NIV).

Being transformed by the renewing of our minds is a process that every person must go through to access freedom. This will allow us to put away our own negative and corrupt thinking patterns and put on God's thoughts. Ephesians 4:22-24 (NASB) encourages us to, "put off concerning the former conversations (behaviors) the old self which is corrupt according to the deceitful lusts; and be renewed in the spirit of our mind; and that we put on the new self, which God created in righteousness and true holiness.

We must do our part in healing our soul wounds, as God does His part within us.

How do we renew our minds?

1. Read the Bible daily. Start with Psalms and St. John. Allow the word of God to work in you. The word of God is living and powerful; it will comfort you, heal you and it will set your soul free. We cannot renew our minds without reading the word. There must be an exchange of information and the exchange is our old thinking (learned behaviors that is contrary to God) with a new way of thinking (the word), so that we can develop the mind of Christ.

   Work out your salvation with fear and trembling, for it is God who is at work in you, both to will and to work for His good pleasure. Philippians 2:13 (NASB)

2. Memorize scripture. Psalms 119:11 (NKJV) provides us with key reasons as to why memorizing scripture is so important. "I

have hidden your word in my heart that I might not sin against thee." When we memorize scriptures, it's not so that we can impress people but so that we can be reactive to sin and the challenges that we will face in life.

Memorizing scriptures gives us a reservoir of word to draw from in our times of need, without new word/s we revert back to our old ways and language.

3. Apply the word in your day-to-day life. Allow the word of God to change you. Remember don't revert back to your old way of doing things, do something different.

   Example: You're having a problem with a co-worker and your usual response would be to argue with them. Now you're going to walk away to reevaluate the situation and pray. Mathew 5:44 (NASB) says to, "Love your enemies and pray for those that persecute you." Matthew 5:9 (NASB) says, "Blessed are the peacemakers, for they shall be called the children of God."

   When we use self-control in an area where we didn't before, people will notice and so will God. Let your light shine before men in such a way that they may see your good works and glorify your Father who is in heaven. Matthew 5:16 (NASB)

4. Purposely set your mind on the things that are above.

Think on what's true, honest, just, pure, lovely; things of good report and that are praise worthy. We must choose to live with this mindset. It does not automatically happen. It will take consistency and patience with yourself.

Looking at life through God's perspective and seeking what He desires will change your mind and eventually your life.

Remember as a man thinks, so is he; what you think about will be.

5. Prayer helps us stay connected to God throughout our day. Ask God to help you think good thoughts. Ask Him to guard your heart and teach you how to speak His truth throughout your day. Ask God to tame your tongue, so that you only say what he would be pleased with.

   Here is one of my favorite scriptures to pray:

   Let the words of my mouth, and the meditations of my heart, be acceptable in thy sight, O Lord, my strength and my redeemer. Psalm 19:14 (NASB)

6. Speak life. We reveal the depths of our hearts by the words of our mouths. Out of the abundance of our hearts, the mouth speaks. We cannot speak what is not already in our heart. This

is why we must guard our heart to make sure nothing negative is being planted.

> Death and life are in the power of the tongue, and those who love it will eat its fruit. The words we speak can either kill our dreams, slaughter our self-esteem and destroy our future or they can breathe life on our dreams, give us confidence about who we are in Christ and build an amazing future for us.
>
> We can likewise, speak life into other people's lives as well, by being conscious about what we say and how we say it. If your words are not going to build up a person, keep them to yourself.

The best thing that we can do is allow God to do a mighty work on the inside of us, so that we can think like He thinks and experience the plans that He has for us. When we renew our minds, we learn the perfect will of God for our lives. Then we are able to find purpose and rest for our souls.

Renewing your mind, will change your life.

Healing takes discipline, patience, and more importantly, help from the Holy Spirit. The Holy Spirit is here to help us and to convict us when we operate in error. This means if you say something wrong, or think a negative thought, it's the Holy Spirit inside of you that will ask you, "Why did you think that or why did you say that?" Allow Him to guide and teach you to do things the right way.

Remember, you did not get where you are overnight. The journey to healing is not easy, and at times you will feel like giving up. Don't give up, your healing is too important.

Your wounds are your responsibility and you have to be willing to leave your pain behind so that you can experience an abundant life filled with peace, joy and purpose.

CHAPTER 7

NOW, IT'S TIME TO THRIVE!

"So if the Son makes you free, you will be free indeed" John 8:36 (NASB)

It is God's desire for us to be set free, whole and thriving in what He has created us to do. He wants us to live a life that is prosperous, in good health, even as our soul prospers. Our souls prospers when we renew our minds to God's Word. Our will prospers, when we come into proper alignment under His mission or will for our life. When we heal our minds and submit our will to God's will, we learn His ways and character and we began to put our hope and trust in Him. Our faith increases and we become mature. Instead of becoming emotional about our trials, we wield our swords (the word), this is how our emotions prosper.

As we spend time with God in His word and in prayer, our choices and behaviors will become more and more in line with how God wants us to live. This is how we become a complete and whole person in spirit, soul and body. The goal of healing and dealing with our soul wounds is so that we can go on to wholeness. On this journey, He changes us into His glorious image.

Now the Lord is the Spirit, and where the Spirit of the Lord is, there is liberty or emancipation from bondage and true freedom. And we all, with unveiled face, continually seeing as in a mirror the glory of the Lord, are progressively being transformed into His image from one degree of glory to even more glory, which come from the Lord who, is the Spirit. 2 Corinthians 3:17-18 (AMP)

A Transformed Life

Healing brings a transformation. Healing by the word of God washes off the old stains and residue to change us from the inside out. Healing transforms our minds from the old, ungodly ways of thinking into a new, godly mindset. When our thinking is transformed our behavior (reactions and attitudes) will also follow. Then our speech will be different. Our mind is how we think, our will is what we do and our emotions is how we express what we are thinking. These all should be transformed for the better. When our soul is healed we are able to make better decisions, react to stressful events in life better and we should be able to govern our emotions; temperance.

With healing, there should be evidence that other people can see. They should take notice of our loving ways: our joy, the peace that we walk in, our patience and self-control when we are dealing with stressful issues.

I was in my twenties, when I went through another stage on my healing journey. I had a nasty attitude; I would say and do whatever I wanted to say and do. I didn't care if it hurt other people, because I was hurting on the inside, "Hurting people hurt other people." When I tell people about my old self, they sometimes have a hard time believing me. What changed me? I had to give my hurt and rejection to God. I had to embrace the truth of His word and allow God to begin His work in me.

Now, I realize that I do care and I don't want to be the responsible of someone else's soul wound.

Healing brings a change of heart, renewed mindset, modified behavior and a godly attitude. The good news of the gospel heals our afflictions, mends our broken hearts, so that our souls can be set free from the condition that it's in. When God heals us through the washing of His word, He exchanges our ashes for beauty, he anoints our heads with the oil of joy and He clothes us with the garment of praise. We are changed from the inside out, with evidence.

Our appearance and attitude will exude the change that has taken place on the inside. I can testify to this. I have a picture of myself from when I was about 22 years old. In this picture, I was clearly depressed. My complexion was darker and I looked older. Today, my complexion is lighter and I think I look younger than I did when I was going through that season of depression. Prayer and yielding to the will of God changes us from the inside out.

And while He was praying, the appearance of His face became different and His clothing became white and gleaming. Luke 9:29 (NASB)

It's our responsibility to maintain our healing.

Healing our wounds is our responsibility and so is maintaining the healing we receive and our continued growth. Healing is a life-long journey. As long as we live on earth, there will be opportunities to be wounded again. But with a renewed mindset and the word of God, our souls should never return to the condition that it was in. We must do the work to maintain our healing.

Through my healing journey, I have learned some valuable and necessary boundaries that I need in my life to maintain my healing. Setting healthy boundaries is not selfish but is important and these boundaries should not be compromised.

My relationship with God is my number one priority. He is the one who balances everything in my life. My peace, my joy and my time are by products of my relationship with Him and these things are what I call non-negotiable. The people I keep in my inner circle are necessary for me to thrive in my marriage, raising my sons, on my job and in my God ordained purpose; these boundaries help me keep my life balanced.

What does it mean to be at peace?

Well, let's start with what peace is not. Peace is not the absence of conflict, stress or the absence of troubles. It is not a temporary escape from conflict. Peace is wholeness; completeness or a soul at rest. Peace is not the absence of troubles, but the ability to be unmoved by the troubles. Our peace is empowered through our relationship with God.

We can look at Jesus's life and find peace. As hard as some of us have had it, none of us have had to face death every day, and none of us are facing a brutal death on a cross. Jesus did. Even when Jesus was preparing for the most stressful and conflicted moment in His life, He was teaching and ministering to His disciples about peace. How abnormal is that? How could He be at peace even when He was about to face a brutal crucifixion? He understood the Peace of God. He not only knew it, but He lived it.

The Peace of God is not found in our environment. It has no relation to the state of worldly affairs or our marriage, children, health or our job status. The Peace of God cannot be externally produced through exercise, drugs or shopping. These only provide temporary experiences of peace. The Peace of God goes beyond our futile capabilities and thinking. It's not reproducible by our human efforts.

The Peace of God comes from our faith in trusting who God is.

FAITH is:

F - Fully

A - Accepting the

I - Inner peace

T - That comes from trusting your

H - Heavenly Father

When we trust God we fully accept the inner peace that comes from trusting Him. We can rest, knowing that whatever we face in life was always out of our control in the first place. God's will for us is better than what we could have done. Knowing this gives us peace, so that we can rest and allow God's will and plan to work out for us. We don't have to strive for this, but we allow the Peace of God to rest upon us.

How do we do this?

We repent for thinking of ourselves and in our abilities, instead of God's way. Repentance puts us back in right relationship with God. Being in right relationship, puts us at ease and makes us at peace with God, so that we can trust Him to protect us, provide for us and heal us. Our trust in Him, keeps us from worry, stress, anxiety and fear. Trusting God means that we believe in Him and His ability to provide whatever it is that we need in this life and the one to come.

We must fully accept the inner peace that flows from God, so that it can transform us from within and change our outer life. This peace keeps our hearts and our minds through Christ Jesus.

The Peace of God causes us to rise above the expected normal reactions or dissatisfactions of life. This peace is supernatural because it's outside our capabilities. None of our efforts will be sufficient.

Our peace and joy are directly related, they both come from our God. In John 14:27 (NASB), Jesus leaves us with His peace that cannot be given by the world. In John 15, it tells us that if we stay connected to Jesus, the true vine then His joy will be in us and that joy will be made full.

Let's clarify something. Joy and happiness are not the same. Happiness is expressed externally and is dependent on what's happening to us or around us. Joy is internal. It is a state of being, meaning it already is. Joy is an attitude of the heart and spirit that's already on the inside of us.

When we keep God at the center of our life (spiritual life and physical body), we are able to tap into His reservoir of peace and strength and anything else we need, to live a thriving and abundant life on earth.

Your joy, peace and time are as priceless as your soul. Our time here on earth is so short that we must be careful how we spend it. Once it's over, it's over.

How you live this life and who you decide to do life with are equally important. If we can't walk in agreement with each other, we can't walk together. There will be times where you have to agree to disagree but this should not be the norm, but the exception. Relationships that are full of strife, contention, confusion and antagonism are too expensive. Romans 12:18 (NKJV) tells us, "If it is possible, as much as depends on you, live peaceably with all men." This means, sometimes it's not possible to live in peace with certain people. Cut your losses and find people who live by your standards and who value what you value. Disconnecting from toxic and dysfunctional people is a part of having healthy emotional boundaries for your life.

Surround yourself with people who encourage you to be a better person; people who support and love you unconditionally. Surround yourself with people who will tell you the truth and who are able to receive truth, as well. Find people who will pray for you and not prey on you. Surround yourself with people who know your God-given purpose and who will hold you accountable. Having a healthy inner circle, is so necessary to your thriving in an abundant life.

Your life is valuable! Your soul is priceless and your joy and peace are too expensive to allow the issues of life to disturb you. We must guard our hearts (mind) for out of it flows the issues of life. Protect it, don't allow people or things to cause you to forfeit all the hard work it takes to heal.

Healed people love and respect themselves enough to protect their minds, hearts, peace, joy, time and their relationship with God. When we keep Him at the center of everything, He keeps our lives healthy, whole and well balanced.

Find purpose and thrive in it!

Now, it's time to thrive.

I believe that each one of us at some point on our journey in life has asked this question, "Who am I and why am I here?" Well, God is the potter and we are the clay. He created us and made plans for us in advance, so that we would feel fulfilled, whole and complete.

He declares, "For I know the plans that I have for you, plans for welfare and not for calamity to give you a future and a hope. Jeremiah 29: 11 (NASB)

This is one of my favorite scriptures in the Bible. I love it because it gives us a clear picture about what the Father thinks about us. Each one of us can read this scripture and feel His love speaking to our hearts. He says, "I have plans for you". Isn't that amazing? This verse reiterates that we are a forethought and not an afterthought. That word plan means to have a detailed proposal for doing or achieving something, i.e., an idea, a plan of action, a strategy, a schedule or an agenda.

When someone puts you on their schedule or makes plans to carve out their time for you specifically, that means that person is interested in relationship with you. Father God, has made plans for you. He goes on to say, "plans for your welfare i.e., your health, your happiness, your well-being, your security, safety, prosperity; plans for your success. Isn't He such a good, good Father?

We know that with good intentions, even the best plans can be hindered. Bad things do happen to us because we live in this world and we have an enemy who is seeking whom he can devour. God will allow these things in our life to mature us, to make us whole and to produce staying power. This causes us to maintain a commitment despite fatigue and difficulty, so that we will lack nothing as we fulfill our purpose.

God uses all things for His good. We must look at things from His perspective all while keeping our peace. We can count it all joy when we face trials in life. Trials are here to test us and develop us for the task that He has set before us.

Nothing that we have gone through will ever go to waste. Every tear that you have cried was to make you more sensitive and compassionate to another person's pain. The result is you will be able to relate to them and encourage them to keep going and let them know that things will get better. We can tell them our story to help them along their journey.

Every pain that you've endured, will be used for your purpose. God will extract good out of every negative situation: the abuse and injustice you suffered, that addiction and/or compulsive behavior, the miscarriage, the death of a child, the divorce, the loss of a job, the sickness you suffered or the fact that you were born an orphan; abandoned or rejected by your parents. Are all painful events that could have destroyed us and for some of us it did, for a minute. But we overcame these things so that we could testify to another person of how we overcame. You see we are not here for ourselves. We are here to help someone else come out of their life's challenges; like we did.

We overcome by the blood of the lamb and the word of our testimony, and they did not love their life even when faced with death. Revelations 12:11 (NASB)

Your life is your ministry. To minister means to serve; to give help to or to take care of. You do not have to be an ordained minister to minister to someone else. Ministering is giving what you have to someone who needs it. Your life and everything that you have gone through, added with the word of God, ministers to someone else's soul. Being vulnerable and healed from our past secret hurts will save someone else from the difficulties that we faced or help someone come out of the bondage that they are in.

Who is more equipped to guide someone through the healing process of child abuse, than someone who has experienced child abuse? Who is better equipped to help an addict get clean and stay clean than an ex- addict? Who is better equipped to help a single mother navigate raising children and managing a household than a single mother who has done it? Whatever your 'ex' is, you are equipped to help someone who is currently going through that struggle in their life. God takes our pain, our failures and our brokenness to use them as testimonies.

God uses our pain for purpose. When we heal our wounds, we find out who we really are (identity) and what we are here to do (purpose). What the devil meant for evil, God will use for good, if we allow Him to. All of us have been a victim of something. If you are still alive, you've survived it but there is still one more step that we must move into - thriving.

For a long time, I was in survivor mode and many of you are just surviving right now. Survivor mode is just existing; just healed enough to get by, but not enjoying a life of peace and joy. You're stagnant and living a life that is not fulfilling.

I understand.

I suppressed my past and barely thought or talked about any of the things that I'd been through. Until recently, I was still just going with the flow of life: going to work, raising kids and being a wife. Every now and then I would step into ministry by encouraging another woman by telling her my truth.

I recently took a sabbatical from work, so that I could do ministry and write this book. During this time, I was invited to speak at a women's empowerment event. The topic that I was asked to speak about was, "Overcoming Tragedy and Pain". At first, I was dumbfounded and maybe even offended by that word tragedy. I thought, "I haven't had any tragedies in my life", so I had to research what tragedy was.

A tragedy is an event that caused great suffering, destruction and distress, such as a serious accident, crime or natural catastrophe. It's a calamity, trial, tribulation, an affliction or a disappointment.

After studying, I was able to relate this word "tragedy," to my life. I say this to show you how stuck I was in survivor mode. We sometimes celebrate the fact that we are survivors. We sing the song. We put stickers on our cars. We ring the bells to signify that we survived cancer. There is absolutely nothing wrong with these things. Yes, we should celebrate, but all too often we stay in survivor mode because it's comfortable and just too painful to revisit what we have come through.

I was there. After I researched the word tragedy, I thought about what I wanted to share with the women who were coming to this event. I decided that I would share how I overcame rejection. I knew this story oh, so well, that I didn't sit down to actually write notes and think through what I would say until 2 days before the event. As I sat down, I tried to put the words on paper but I kept getting a nudge from the Holy Spirit to share with them the sexual abuse that I went through. I adamantly rejected that option, but I heard this, "You don't get to decide what you will or will not talk about. You will say what I want you to say." As a minister of the gospel, we don't get to speak about what we feel we should say but what He says. As I sat at my desk, I began to weep uncontrollably. I mean I was a snooty mess. This is when I realized that I was not completely healed from the abuse. I felt shame and the fear of telling my secret to an audience grip me.

As I wept, I heard the Lord say, "It's time to thrive." But, what does that mean? I was thriving, so I thought. I had the career, the house, the car I wanted. We traveled. I had a nice savings account and was married with children. I'm living the "American Dream." But if I were honest with myself, I did not feel fulfilled, I was just going through the motions of an ordinary life. None of these things satisfied me. No matter how many trips, clothes, shoes or how much money I had, it wasn't enough.

There was a void, a yearning for something more. You see, our relationships, careers, substances, material possessions or even accolades will not fill our void. The only thing that will fill that void is being at peace with God, and finding and thriving in what God has purposed us for.

This is why healing our wounds is such an important step; healing allows us to be free, so that we can find our purpose and it allows us to be open to speaking our truth.

When we thrive, we are free to tell the truth about ourselves by uncovering the secret wounds that once had us bound. When we are truly free from our past, we are free to share the details of our past and expose our secrets *without* guilt or shame.

You see, even though I survived, I still was not free. I was afraid that people would see and judge my wounds. This kept me from being authentic to myself and transparent. People want the truth of who we are and they want to see how you have overcome. Most people are hiding who they truly are due to shame, guilt and fear. They can't talk about their stuff because most aren't healed themselves.

In order to be a deliverer you must first be delivered. Healing and deliverance happens when we are walking in truth and are willing to be transparent. Our transparency, gives hope to our audience, that they too can be healed, delivered and walk in purpose.

The day came that I was to speak about my abuse for the very first time in public. I was so nervous. Actually I was trembling. Thank God, it was a small and intimate venue, where we could all mingle and get acquainted with each other. When I got up, I prayed and began to speak. I felt naked, standing there telling the intimate details of my story; outwardly I looked calm and collected, but on the inside I was terrified. I quickly sat down, not realizing that two women were weeping. I asked, "Why are you crying?" the first woman, who was a 66 year-old retiree, revealed that she had been sexually abused when she was 10 years-old and had never told anyone for 55 years. She said because of my boldness, she felt strong enough to tell her truth today. The other woman asked, "What if you told your mother, but she didn't believe you?" Oh my God, I didn't expect this. I was caught up trying to process my feelings and overcome my fear that I wasn't prepared for people to respond to my story.

Sometimes we get so focused on what we are going through, that we can't see who we are called to. We overly think that we have to have every moment planned out. But in reality, we just have to be bold enough to be transparent.

When I left there, I could see the purpose for God wanting me to speak my truth. He needed me to be completely healed from my past, so that I could move from surviving to thriving, from complacency into purpose and fulfilment. He had a greater need for my story that day. It was bigger than me and anybody else in that room. He knew each person who would be in attendance on that day. Even if they weren't strong enough to speak their truth right then, but because they saw me do it, one day they would find the strength to uncover their secret wounds and speak their truth.

If we don't allow God to use what we have been through for good, the devil will use it against us for evil. God's plans and ways are better than anything that we could think of or imagine. When we seek Him and His righteousness, all things will be added; we will never lack anything and we will live a life that is fulfilled.

I encourage you as I encourage myself to allow God to heal you, set you free from all bondages. Then ask God what His plan is for your life, pursue it and thrive in it.

Things to remember:

- Uncover your secret wounds by being open and honest with yourself.
- Remember a part of the definition for secret is to close mouths; don't be silenced by fear, guilt and shame but free yourself from the self-imposed prison.
- Secrets kill us spiritually, physically, emotionally and they rob us from having healthy intimate relationships.
- Secrets cripple us, so that we never fulfill our purpose or live in freedom.
- Healing is an individual responsibility; you may not be responsible for how you got your wounds but you are responsible for your healing.

Healing is an act of self-care and love. Accept your flaws and failures and love yourself enough to allow yourself space to heal. Someone has need of what you have on the inside of you. Don't just be a survivor, go thrive!

ABOUT THE AUTHOR

Jameka Turner is thriving in her life with her husband and two sons. She was born and raised in Northwest Indiana. She loves reading, studying the Bible, teaching and writing. She loves spending time with family, listening to music and watching movies. She loves to travel; her bags are always half packed! She loves God. She lives a life of prayer and intercession. She loves being in the presence of God. She lives by the motto, "audience of one." She has a heart for the wounded and broken. Her desire is to see people healed, delivered and living life on purpose, to glorify God.